ALONE IN DESERT PLACES

Richard C. Fennell, D.D., Th.D.

Order this book online at www.trafford.com
or email orders@trafford.com

Most Trafford titles are also available at major online book retailers.

Print information available on the last page.

ISBN: 978-1-5539-5717-1 (sc)
ISBN: 978-1-4122-5322-2 (e)

Cover Village of Dei, Sudan
Photographs taken by Richard C. Fennell, D.D., TH.D

Trafford rev. 06/18/2021

North America & international
toll-free: 844-688-6899 (USA & Canada)
fax: 812 355 4082

CONTENTS

4

1

LAND OF THE BLUE NILE

Africa was only a dream, a world away, as I challenged myself to go there. Exotic land of enchantment, where opportunities are endless, as dreams are made or broken. I wanted an adventure that would last a lifetime, and decided to apply for foreign employment. The resumes seemed endless, as I tried fervently to contact foreign employers. The days turned into weeks without a single reply. I decide to be relentless in my pursuit, leaving no stone unturned. With dreams of Kenya, Mozambique, and the Congo, I address resumes to the 2nd largest continent on earth.

Dreams of Africa were soon to become a reality as the phone rings at 2 A.M. It must be a wrong number I thought. No one would be calling this time of the morning. I decide to answer on the 5th ring and a voice called me by name.

"Hello, did you make application for foreign employment?"

"Yes, who is this?" I asked.

"I'm calling from Khartoum, Sudan. I'll call a local travel agency in your city and purchase a round trip ticket. They'll contact you later today. I want you to fly to Khartoum, Sudan. We'll have someone meet you upon arrival. We'll answer your questions at that time," and abruptly hangs up.

Not knowing where Sudan was located, I began to look at a world map. I notice it is a large, arid country located in North Africa. I'd prefer to go into the dense jungle region of Central Africa for adventure. I'll take this job because it is a step in the right direction. I began to pack everything I could get into a large suitcase. At nine A.M. sharp the phone rings again.

"Hello sir. We have a round trip ticket for you. You can pick it up before 5 o'clock."

Arriving at the travel agency, I'm handed a round trip ticket stamped, "Destination Khartoum, Sudan, total price $1966.58." I didn't have a clue about wages, only they had invested a lot of money in me. The caller never mentioned the job description, only to fly to this destination. I decided I couldn't go wrong with a round trip ticket. If things don't work out, I'll fly back to the United States and try again. I return home and begin to tie up all loose ends and prepare for an opportunity of a lifetime.

Walking into the Atlanta airport is quite intimidating. I had flown into one of the nation's busiest airports from the small Pine belt regional airport in Hattiesburg, MS. Its busy terminal is nonstop, as travelers from around the world merge inside her busy corridors. I have a 4 hour layover as I anxiously awaited to crawl aboard the Lufthansa 747 jumbo jet en-route to Frankfurt, Germany.

Taking my passport and oversized suitcase, I decide to go through U.S. Customs and wait for the flight to arrive from Europe. I had plenty of time to think about backing out.

I began to weigh my options. Maybe this was my only offer for overseas employment. I decided not to question it any longer. I'll remain optimistic and look forward to my new assignment.

A voice rang out " Lufthansa flight 429M now boarding, nonstop to Frankfurt, Germany." I take my boarding pass and stand in line with over 200 passengers. In a matter of minutes the huge aircraft was loaded to full capacity. I sit quietly, as we listen to the instructions of the flight attendant.

Within minutes the aircraft taxied out upon the runway. The giant engines began to roar as we became airborne for the trans-Atlantic flight. The jumbo jet climbed, ever so slowly, as we feel turbulence in the body of the aircraft. Climbing to over 30,000 feet, the aircraft became smooth, as we began the long journey to Europe. Looking out the window, only darkness prevailed, as it surrounded the aircraft. The somber mood of the passengers became contagious, as everyone nestled into sleep.

"Please fasten your seat belts and place your seats into the up right position as we prepare to land." rang out, as the flight attendants ran to and fro the aircraft.

We're on approach to land in Frankfurt, Germany. The aircraft slowed, as we began our descent into the cold skies over Germany. Looking from the window, I see the snow covered roofs of buildings and homes. Within minutes the aircraft comes to a complete halt, in the center of the tarmac, approximately 200 yards from the terminal. Several men and women began pushing a ramp in our direction. I began to wonder what could possibly be happening. Suddenly, the captains voice rang out over the intercom.

"Please exit the aircraft and walk toward the terminal. Please be patient and take your time." This was quiet different from previous flights I had made. Walking down the temporary stairs I notice the presence of armed guards and police. We walk single file toward the terminal. Long streams of yellow police tape wrap around a large section of the airport.

We're surrounded by military personnel with assault weapons, wearing black uniforms and helmets. The quietness was overwhelming as the tension began to build. We're taken through customs and physically searched. One by one, we enter a small booth to be frisked and pass through metal detectors. Once inside the terminal, we notice a large area had been closed. I approach a ticket counter that is surrounded by armed guards and police. A strong overwhelming smell of gun powder and smoke is present.

A very nervous ticket agent asked," Can I help you sir?"

"Yes, can you tell me what has happened to your terminal?"

"We had a large explosion early this morning, and we're trying to get back to normal." she stated.

"What caused the explosion?" I asked.

"We believe a bomb was left in a tote bag, but no one knows for sure."

I turn and walk toward the corridor to get a better look. I was stopped immediately, by armed guards who warned me to stay away. I turn and walk to the opposite end of the airport and wait for my next flight. It'll be aboard another Lufthansa aircraft. I have a 13 hour layover, as I anxiously await to continue my journey.

I return to the waiting area and notice a large burly man of English decent. A small sign on his brief case read "United Export Services." I decide to walk over and strike up a conversation.

"Where are you going sir?"

"England. I'm returning home after a trip to Kenya." he said.

"Were you on business or vacation?"

"Both actually. I buy and sell curios, and Kenya has a variety of them." he said.

"Do you travel all of Africa?"

"No. I travel to South Africa mainly, in the winter months, and Kenya and Central Africa in the summer."

"How long have you been doing this?" I asked.

"Over twenty years and it's a fabulous job. I can't think of anything I'd rather do. What's your destination?"

"Khartoum, Sudan." I said.

"Are you with one of the relief agencies?" he asked.

"I'm not sure what you mean by a relief agency."

"Sudan is in a severe famine at this time. Millions of people are affected and various relief agencies are in a battle to save the starving masses. I thought you may be affiliated with this program now underway."

Before I could speak another word, a voice rang out overhead, "British Air flight BA0226 to London, now boarding."

"Here's my card. I'm John Holland and if you're ever in

the U.K., look me up."

He walked about 10 paces and turned, saying in a serious voice, "Be careful, Sudan is a very dangerous place."

"I will, thanks."

I began to think about the dangers that might lie ahead. Maybe, I would be with some type of relief effort. I had no experience in this field and began to wonder why I would even be considered for this type of employment. I could not think of anything on my resume that would qualify me for this. It didn't matter at this point. I was halfway to Khartoum, and nothing short of death would keep me away. I only wish I could have gotten more information on the famine. I decide to return to the gate that would board the final flight before reaching Khartoum.

The hours passed ever so slowly, as I sat waiting for the flight to arrive. I notice the number of people en-route to Sudan had dwindled. Only a handful of people present, and nearly all were en-route to Cairo, Egypt. Everyone present were Arabs, as I sat listening to them speak in their native tongue.

Suddenly, it's announced that Lufthansa Flight 538 from Frankfurt to Cairo and Khartoum is preparing to board. The departure time is 1:40 P.M. with an arrival time of 9:20 P.M. in Khartoum. I wait for the aircraft to approach the terminal, but it stopped over 200 meters from the building. We're told to walk onto the tarmac, pick-up our own luggage, and board the aircraft. One by one, we hand our luggage to an agent to be placed inside the storage compartment, and then board the plane. Sitting alone, are three pieces of luggage no one had claimed. It is wheeled away back inside a small underground storage room. Within minutes, we're airborne once again, with only a small group of passengers. A flight attendant walks over and began speaking to me in German.

"I'm an American." I said.

"Sorry sir, you looked German," she said.

It became very silent as we settle in for the long flight. I have plenty of time to gather my thoughts about what the Englishman had told me about the famine in Sudan.

I try to sleep but it escapes me. I'm getting nervous as the hours begin to pass and we're getting closer to my destination. After 8 hours in the air we begin our approach Cairo, Egypt. Within minutes, we're on the ground, and the plane is empty. Two passengers came aboard and we're in the air once again for the hour flight to Khartoum.

I'm become apprehensive thinking about what I'm getting into. The plane began turning as we circle the city. I look out the window and see thousands of lights on the ground.

Touchdown, and we're approaching the terminal. The plane comes to a halt, and we exit the aircraft into a dimly lit room with men dressed in military fatigues. I walk to the front of the line and hand the officer my passport. He looks it over twice and asked for my visa. I stand there dumb-founded and say, " I don't understand what you mean."

"YOUR PASSPORT DOESN'T HAVE A VISA!" he shouted.

"What are you doing here?" asked the other officer.

"I'm going to work." I answered nervously.

"Who are you going to work for?"

"I don't know. I was told to report here and someone would meet me at this airport."

"It's 9:30 P.M. Nobody is going to come here tonight. Stand over in that corner, and we'll see if anyone comes for you."

I watch as the 2 military officers began searching my suitcase. Opening it, they pick up my King James Bible, and lay it to one side. Taking out all my belongings, they search the small pockets. Finding nothing of interest, they replace everything, placing it to one side. Keeping my passport they began speaking Arabic and laughing. I knew someone would show up but when. I'll wait until daylight to see what happens. I grew very weary and hungry, past the point of exhaustion. The hours were dragging past without a word being spoken. Only occasional glances, and then laughing.

The flies were swarming and the night air became bone chilling as the night wore on. Daylight finally makes its welcome appearance. I see a Sudanese man approaching the 2 officers. He briefly spoke to the military men, turned and approached me.

"Are you Mr. Richard?" he asked.

"Yes, yes." I answered.

"Come go with me."

We approach the two officers and they hand the man my passport and suitcase. Leaving the terminal was a sigh of relief. I felt like I had been imprisoned my first night in the Sudan.

"Who are you?" I asked.

"I have been sent for you." he answered.

"Where are we going?"

"I will take you to your quarters." he said.

We stop in front of a small, dirty and empty building.

The driver exits the car, grabs my bag, and walked into a small room. Suddenly, he turns saying, "Wait here, someone will be come for you very shortly."

"What about my passport?"

"I will keep it and get a Visa stamp inside for you." He said walking out the door.

I begin to worry at this point. I'm in a strange land, without my passport. I've gone 24 hours without food or sleep. I sat down and waited for someone to appear. I felt like a complete fool as I sat, waiting.

Suddenly, a knock at the door, and in walks a small Sudanese woman .

"I'm going to cook breakfast for you" she said in broken English.

"Yes, please, by all means."

I back out of the way, as she kills a small chicken and begins to pluck the feathers. She started a fire and cooked the chicken and presented it to me. Without hesitation, I begin to eat everything she had cooked. I was glad to get anything to eat at this point. As she started to leave I asked her. "Is someone going to take me to the office?"

"Yes, soon very soon." she says before leaving.

I sat down and started to drift into deep sleep when another knock came at the door. Opening the door, a small Sudanese man tells me to follow him.

"What about my bag?" I asked.

"It's O.K., leave here." he said in broken English.

I follow close behind, as we walk 2 blocks and enter a small 2 story building. A number of women are working as secretaries, and one tells me to sit down at her desk. She's not Sudanese, but Philippino.

"I want you to fill out this piece of paper and then someone will see you." she said.

I began to fill out the paperwork and anxiously await my fate.

"He will see you now." she said.

I walk into a rather modest office and saw an American with ruddy complexion. He was a little over 6 feet tall, stern faced with mustache, beard and slightly overweight.

"Hello Richard, How was your trip?" he asked.

"It was excellent." I answered.

"I'm glad you came."

"I'm happy to be here. What's my new assignment?"

"I need for you to go into the remote region of Western Darfur province of Sudan, and run a road building job. You'll be the Field Supervisor for Arkel-Talab. You'll be in charge of 2 African construction companies in that area. Your job will be to build pioneer roads in a region, with no roads, so we can get emergency food shipments moving in that area. It is a rough area with no power or basic necessities. It'll take some getting use to but I know you will adapt. Do you have any questions?"

"Yes sir. When do I leave?" I asked.

"Tomorrow morning, and I'll keep in contact with you." he said as he escorted me to the door.

I had the experience to build the roads, so I'll go and do a good job for the Sudanese people. I want to do my part in getting the food into the hard to reach areas and save lives. This'll be a great challenge for me. I'll become relentless in my pursuit to accomplish this mission.

14

The following morning, rising early, I anxiously wait to get underway. I didn't have long to wait before a Sudanese driver arrives.

"Are we going to the airport?" I asked.

"No, we're going to a storage area so you can see where the food shipments will be coming from." he said.

We arrive at the Khartoum distribution center. The sacks of food were stacked in large piles for several acres. I see hundreds of workers standing around, and none of the food is being moved.

I walk through thousands of bags of food that were sitting, and beginning to rot. I couldn't understand why there weren't any trucks being loaded at this time. The flies were swarming so thickly it was difficult to breath.

"Why isn't this food being moved today?" I asked.

"The railroad is broken down for hundreds of miles. The rainy season has began to cut off more than 3 million people in Darfur Province who desperately need the food. Wet food is sitting around, rotting in sacks. Only a tenth of the food needed will arrive unless something is done very soon." he said.

The crack of a bullwhip can be heard, as the guards began chasing starving beggars away from the food. Young and old alike, were beginning to flee, as the guards chased away the hungry. I was disappointed in the operation that was currently going on.

No doubt, it could be better if someone was in command. I was angered by the lack of concern for getting the food moving. It was apparent the food relief operation had bogged down at the local level in Sudan. Thousands of children will die as a result of these failed efforts. Sudan, with an area size of the United States east of the Mississippi river, faces a catastrophic famine.

With a population of around 22 million, over 3.5 million face death in the next few months. The port and railhead is over flowing with food sitting idle, while no one seems to be in charge. The American people had answered the call for help and responded with over 800 million dollars in aid.

At least 3,500 trucks would be necessary to move the food into every area of Sudan. It would take 15 days to cross the harsh sub-Saharan desert. At least 1,800 tons a day must be moved in order to meet the very minimum requirements for survival.

A trip from Khartoum to Nyala is approximately 600 miles of rough terrain. Roads are almost non-existent and the railroad is practically a thing of the past. Sudan now faces a nightmare, as well as those who seek to save them. We're just starting what I thought we should be finishing. It would take an act of God to prevent the millions from dying, especially those in the far away Darfur Province.

Sudan, with the worst drought and food shortage in its history, is in shambles. A 30 year war against its own people in the southern region results in half the grain never reaching its destination. Many of the trucks are being robbed along the way by bandits. The Sudanese army refuses to use its trucks for the relief effort, saying they lack fuel. The United States has supplied the fuel, but it is now mostly unaccounted for. It is quiet evident the Sudanese government accounts for nothing.

Much of the money sent to Sudan has been misappropriated by top officials. There were projects designed to create new jobs but instead were used to build houses. Trees are being cut as fuel to bake bread, leaving starving people to sell charcoal as their only source of income.

Sudan's open border has allowed over 1.5 million refugees from Ethiopia and Chad to enter, causing an even greater demand for food. All food, medical services, shelter and transportation is being paid by western donors. The United States alone has given more than 100 million tons of food.

Most of it sits idle before me, as I watch in disbelief of the little effort made to distribute it. Private truck owners are bidding higher and higher, trying to make a large profit delivering the food. It has been reported that over 300,000 tons of food has been buried by merchants until the price rises. Greed has taken precedence over life.

"What is the Sudanese Government contributing to the famine relief?" I asked.

"We are providing the land to store the food and charge no taxes." answered the driver.

Khartoum, a river junction of the Blue and White Nile, is a melting pot of many people. It's very name means "Elephant Trunk", because the shape of the Nile River resembles the trunk of an elephant at this junction. The dusty, dirt roads and brown colors of small shanties amid a city of low scale homes stretch for miles.

Dark skin men dressed in white, sitting in doorways, seem almost sedated. Laid back with the appearance of not a single worry. All the basic things we take for granted are non-existent. It looks like a ghost town, with an abundance of people.

Stop and ask for directions, only to be met with the phrase "No English." Nothing is done today, only "BOOK-RAH", or tomorrow.

Arabic is the basic language, but you soon find more than 400 dialects being spoken. The northern areas of the Sudan are Muslim, with a relative few Christians. The largest group of Christians live in southern Sudan and are currently at war with the north. If the people of Sudan are to be saved from death, it will be because of the westerners who have came to the rescue.

I see a number of land rovers with names like Oxfam, Doctors without Borders, UNICEF and Save The Children. Australia, Great Britain, Ireland, Germany and many other European Nations have contributed to the relief. The United States has provided the bulk of the food to be distributed. Each group seems to be operating independently, which makes the operation and even greater challenge.

"It is time to catch your flight. We'll go now." said the driver.

We arrive at the airport at 10 A.M. and find a small Nile Safari aircraft. A Sudanese pilot greets us and carries my bag aboard. The sun is extremely bright, with not a cloud in the sky. The temperature is rising as the small plane begins to heat up inside. Within minutes, we are underway to a destination unknown to me. I only know that it is in a very remote area of Western Darfur Province. I'll be exiting the aircraft in a small town known as Nyala. I pull a small pocket calendar from my brief case and mark the date, July 1, 1985.

Looking down from the sky, I see nothing short of a scorched, red earth, without inhabitant. The ground has a burnt orange and reddish tint that looks almost impenetrable on foot. It is a mass of dead trees, rocks, and sand without any sign of water. It appears that the country is just a means of holding Chad to Ethiopia, and not suitable for any living creature.

Heading due west, the terrain below appears to be getting worse. I notice a small town begins to appear on the horizon. It's in a very remote area of the desert. Landing on a tiny air strip we approach a small building with a sign that reads, "El Obeid."

We exit the aircraft, enter the small terminal, and are greeted by local merchants. I'm the only white man present, which brings plenty of stares. The pilot informed me, we'll refuel, and be out of here in about an hours' time.

This is a very dry, dusty area that transports water into the city to survive. The area has little to offer those who pass this way. A sandstorm is pelting the area, as we take shelter inside a small building.

We stay put until the storm passes, and we're in the air once again. I'm excited knowing we're within a couple of hours of Nyala. I continue to look down from the sky upon the reddish sand that supports little life. This is a very harsh area with no visible signs of water or wildlife. Nothing appears to be moving in the desert heat as we soar high above.

2

THE AWAKENING

The pilot points directly ahead as he prepares for landing. We fly over a small building in the city, bank to the left, and approach a small airport. Within minutes, we're on the ground and exit the aircraft. I see small huts and people dressed in white clothes, walking in every direction. Suddenly, a land rover appears and a white man hops out and introduces himself.

"Hello, I'm Ronnie, your contact in Nyala."

"How did you know we were here?" I asked.

"The pilot always does a fly-over when he has cargo." he said.

I load my bag and we are en-route to the Arkel-Talab office. We weave through the tiny dirt streets. The villagers are sitting under make shift dwellings, watching as we pass.

We arrive at a small building that has a large wall around it. A Baboon tied to the front gate tries to attack us as we run pass, trying to reach the doorway. A large rope tied to his neck is the only restraining force.

"What is that Baboon doing anyway?" I ask.

"He's the best security guard in town." he said laughing.

"What are you doing out here?" I asked.

"We're trying to coordinate food deliveries into some very remote regions. Your job will be to enter several of these areas and build roads to reach the starving people of Darfur Province. We have a time schedule to meet that has came and gone. We're at least 6-months behind. The rainy season is rapidly approaching and less than 10-percent of the food has reached Nyala. Let's go to the train station and see if a shipment of food has arrived."

Leaving my bags at the small house, we drive through the small dirt roads of Nyala. The streets are lined with people from many parts of Darfur and Chad searching for food. The famine is rampant in all the surrounding areas. Arriving at the train depot, we see a large crowd gathering in search of food.

"Is the train from Khartoum arriving today?" Ronnie asked the railroad agent.

"Yes. In about an hour."

We decide to wait until it arrives. The crowd began to push and shove as the train slowly comes into view. I'm amazed to see the hundreds of people riding on top of the rail cars. Many of them had caught the train from as far away as Khartoum and El Obeid, riding upon the top in the fierce heat, under very harsh conditions. Many of them appear to be exhausted with dehydration. The train stopped, and the crowd began to attack the rail cars housing the food. The police take camel whips and began to beat the crowd back. Many of the starving people endure the whipping and continue to pull the grain from the cars. They began ripping the grain open and grabbing as much as possible before fleeing. Finally the police gain control of the people driving them away from the food. Workers began to fill the transport or "souk" trucks with food as quickly as possible.

"Where will this food be taken?" I asked.

"It will be distributed among the local people and moved into remote villages as the road become available." he said.

"When will I be able to begin the road building?"

"It'll take a few days to get your vehicle running. We found it locally and it has a few problems, including a bad transmission."

"Who's working on it at this time."

"No one. We've hired a philippino mechanic who'll be arriving soon. You'll have to wait until then. It will give you time to rest before heading into the bush."

I was more than a little disappointed. I couldn't rest very well knowing people were dying in this region.

I couldn't believe the lack of transportation was stopping the largest famine relief operation on earth. We are passing through Nyala and I see a new land rover with, Save The Children. Another new vehicle passes with OXFAM printed on the door. These agencies had made prior arrangements to have their transportation in place.

We return to the small Arkel-Talab office, running pass the baboon once again. I open my bag, removing my bible and begin to read. I knew I'd need all the strength I could muster to face what lie ahead. I will walk by faith and not by sight, to meet the new challenges.

Darfur, meaning "House of Fur" and Sudan, Arabic for "Land of Blacks." This remote area of Western Darfur is part of the rugged Sahara and Libyan Desert. It's an immense rolling plain, approximately 170,000 square miles. Other than a few mountain peaks that rise to around 10,000 feet, Darfur is featureless. It is sparsely populated, with stony ground covered by sand, that's constantly being shifted around by changing weather conditions.

Many of the locals are Arab, Furs, Nubian, and Daju. Many of these are large families who have formed their own tribes for centuries. Millet and sorghum are the basic crops grown locally. Goats, sheep, and camels are raised for food and leather.

A number of wadis or seasonal rivers rise in the mountains and flood the plains during heavy rainfall. These are very dangerous, as I would soon find out. Rain comes as a curse and blessing among the villagers of western Darfur. Over 20 years of war and drought have taken its toil on every ethnic group in Sudan. Strict laws govern over the people with an iron fist. There's an abundance of tales of local villagers having their hands amputated for stealing. Another of several women being stoned to death for committing adultery.

Walking with my interpreter through the streets of Nyala, we witness one such punishment. An aid worker from the EEC has been caught with a girl in the act of adultery. We watch in horror as he receives 75 lashes with a camel whip.

He's dragged by the feet to his quarters by 2 policemen. We're told the girl will receive the same punishment.

Slavery, abduction, and forced servitude are a few of the human rights abuses taking place in Sudan. A war between Christian and Muslims has ravaged North and South Sudan for a period of 20 years. These punishments are part of their religion. Amputation is practiced throughout the Islamic world. A report of double amputation {arm & leg} because a thief has been caught twice for stealing, was carried out recently in Nyala.

We walked back to the office, finding the mechanic has arrived to fix the vehicle. It's a 1958 land rover with 4 bald tires. It has to be jump started to crank. He has jacked the vehicle up and began pulling the transmission. It's at least a start in the right direction. I know it'll take a few days before he has it running, because of the lack of spare parts.

"When is the next shipment of food to arrive?" I asked.

"I honestly don't have a clue." Ronnie said.

"I cannot understand why things aren't moving at a faster pace."

"You will find that nothing, nor anyone gets in a hurry in Sudan."

"I want to get out there today, and begin the road building."

"Just take it easy. We'll have you out there soon."

"I want to see a map of the area I'm going into."

"Sorry. I don't have any maps of the area."

"How am I suppose to know where I'm going, if I don't have a map."

"Just ask the villagers and they will direct you into the

areas listed."

"I want to believe this is a real effort to save the masses of starving people. I'm beginning to have doubts now."

"It just takes time to do everything and this is just another obstacle we're trying to overcome."

"I'm not going out there without a map. I'm going down to one of the other relief agencies and ask for one."

"Don't do that, please! They have already blamed us for the food failures."

"Maybe they're right. I don't care about who's right or prestige. I'll return with a map."

Walking out the door and down the street, I traveled several blocks before spotting a vehicle with markings from the EEC. I strolled to the front door and began to knock. A small Sudanese woman opens the door, inviting me inside. It's a rather small office with several European men and women. A bearded man in his late forties walked over and asked if he could be of assistance.

"Yes sir. I need a map of Darfur Province."

"Sure, take a couple of them."

"What relief agency are you with?" he asked.

"Arkel-Talab." I answered.

Without saying another word, he turned and walked away. I could feel resentment, but I had much more to worry about than childish rivalry. Lives were being lost and I'm going to make every effort to do something. I return to the office and began to study the map in great detail. This is a sparsely populated area with few towns and villages. Roads are few in number, with many being mere camel trails.

The following morning, I rise early to check on the

progress of my land rover. Parts are lying in three separate piles. My morale plummeted as the days began to pass ever so slowly. I decided to read my King James Bible, and pray for strength and guidance. Three days passed, before a knock came at the door. Opening it, I find the mechanic smiling, saying,

"Your vehicle is now ready."

I ran out to the land rover to take a look. It still has the bald tires and dead battery. I look around, seeing parts of a Pepsi cola can cut into several pieces.

"What was this used this for?" I asked, pointing at the Pepsi can.

"I used several small pieces in the transmission. It'll last for a while, so don't worry."

I began to believe this was a real dog an pony show now. I will go as far as this ticking time bomb will take me. I grab my bag and load it into the rear of the vehicle.

"Can you jump me off?"

"Sure." he said.

Dragging a pair of jumper cables from his tool box, we managed to crank the land rover. I look at the fuel gage and it is nearly out of fuel. I look around and find 10 gallons of diesel, and pour it into the tank. I couldn't wait any longer to get the road started so the food deliveries could begin. As I began backing out, I noticed someone running toward me.

"Stop!" shouted Ronnie.

"What do you want?"

"Look, it's getting late, and I don't think it would be wise to leave now. A strong rain this morning means the wadi is going to be impassible."

"I'll take my chances with the wadi. I'll find the equipment and be building roads by daylight in the morning. What about a radio so I can keep in touch?"

"Just report back in 7-days and I'll let you know if we can locate you a radio."

"O.K., I'm outta here."

"Don't pick-up any hitch hikers!" he said laughing.

I turn the corner and head down the long, winding, dirt road that leads into the desert. I took the map and began to follow the camel trail as it trekked into the unknown. I drive very slowly through the goats, sheep, and donkeys as the path became very rough and unbelievably remote.

Large rocks, ant hills, and sand dunes covered the area in every direction. I will travel to the wadi to see if it can be crossed after the recent flooding. It'll be about an hours' drive before reaching the crossing. The winds are blowing very hard, as a sandstorm begins to brew. A towering cloud of sand is blowing pellets into the windshield, making it difficult to see.

Without any street signs or roads in the area it is getting very difficult to know if I'm going in the right direction. The dark cloud of sand has engulfed me to the point I'm having difficulty breathing. I begin to drive as slowly as possible, without stopping.

Finally, darkness surrounds me to the point I must stop. I sit with the engine running at a fast idle. I have no way to restart the land rover because of the dead battery. After a few minutes, the storm passes, and I'm on my way again. Looking at the map, the landmarks are getting fewer as I near the barren area halfway to the wadi. Several camels, with riders are passing about 100 meters on my left. After an hours drive, I see the wadi just ahead. I round a small bend in the trail and 6 large souk trucks, loaded with grain, sit idle. I pull along side the first truck as a Sudanese man, waving his hand, asked me to stop.

"Wadi to deep." he said in broken English.

"How long before it's safe to cross?" I asked.

"Maybe book-rah." [Arabic for tomorrow.]

"I can't wait until tomorrow."

"No! book-rah!"

I put the land rover in 4-wheel drive and drove head-first into the fast moving water. I hear the screams of the souk truck drivers on the river bank. The water began rising rapidly, as the drivers seat became wet. I pick a spot on the opposite shore to make landing. I began to say a silent prayer.

The strong current pushed very hard against the small vehicle. I'll have to land in a different spot as the land rover is losing the battle with the swift moving water. I began to fight with the steering wheel to regain control. What seemed like an eternity was only a couple of minutes of sheer misery.

I feel the water starting to recede from beneath the vehicle as I arrive on the opposite side of the wadi. I leave the engine running ,and exit the vehicle to see if the souk trucks will follow. The drivers wave, and laugh as they shout various Arabic words unknown to me. None will follow, and I can't blame them. I'm determined to reach the heavy equipment camped in the desert tonight. I will not rest until I find them.

The small camel trail is quickly beginning to disappear after the sandstorm dumped several inches of sand. The stony ground bounces the vehicle continuously, as I cover as much ground as possible before dark. Another hour has passed and I'm having doubts if I will be successful in finding the camp.

The fuel gage is beginning to fall below the halfway mark. I'll have to make a decision and quickly. I have enough fuel to return to Nyala, if I turn around now. I'll have to cross the wadi, above flood stage once again, if I decide to go back. Darkness is quickly beginning to fall in Western Darfur. I find myself lost, and alone in the desert.

I turn on the head lights and find only one beam working. It's only shining about 10-feet ahead. No sign of a trail remains, so I continue to drive in the direction of the small village of Gyaga, Sudan. It's a mere dot on the map in a vast area of the Sahara Desert.

No sign of life is present as I continue to search with little success. The condition became desperate, as the fuel gage drops to a quarter of a tank. The darkness completely engulfs me, as the headlight begins to grow dim. "Lord, I'm in trouble, please help me," I prayed as I begin to have second thoughts about my decision to continue this journey.

The land rover begins to sputter as the fuel in the bottom of the tank shows signs of water. I have no idea where I'm located, as I continue to head due west.

I'll drive until the fuel runs out, and walk if I have to. It's to late to turn back now, as I face the unknown, alone. I had greatly underestimated the risk I was taking as I entered this remote region. No sign of life can be found as I begin to worry about my future. If I don't find the camp soon I'm going to be stranded in a barren land without food or water. My morale is shattered as I began to think of the foolish decision I had made.

Stopping at the edge of a hill, I leave the land rover idling. I climb as high as possible trying to see anything. Possibly a light in the distance that could give me some direction. Suddenly, in the valley beneath me, a small campfire is burning. My heart pounding, I race to the land rover and drive as quickly as possible in their direction.

I don't care if they're head-hunters, I didn't want to be stranded out here alone. I see the fire growing brighter as I near the site. A walled fence of briars and shrubbery surround the camp, with heavy equipment sitting everywhere. "Thank You, Lord!" I shouted.

Jumping from the vehicle, I ran inside the camp and see dozens of workers running to greet me.

"Quawagi!"[white-man in Arabic], they shouted.

"Hello. Are you Mr. Richard?"

"Yes, yes!" I answered.

"We've been looking for you. Think maybe you no come?" said one of the workers.

"Look fellows, I'm very glad to be here, believe me."

"We have a tent prepared for you."

"Thank you! Thank you!" I said.

"Mr. Richard, my name is Mahdi. I'm the field man for Africa Construction. I'm here to assist you."

"Great. Tell the workers the road building will begin at daylight tomorrow. I will direct you to the job site and we'll go from there."

"Yes sir."

I retire to my quarters, which is a medium size army tent. I'm very happy to be here. It's a miracle that I had found them tonight. I'm thankful to God for directing me to them.

I'll do everything in my power to build the road so the souk trucks can deliver the food to this famine stricken area. Taking my flashlight, I begin going over the map. I'll be ready at first light to get the equipment moving. I drift in and out of sleep in the cool desert air.

Waking early, I hear the prayers of the Muslim faithful. Each has his prayer mat facing toward Mecca, the Holy place of their religion. Each one is praying out loud in Arabic. After a few minutes, each one presents himself to me, letting me know they're ready.

"O.K. Lets get ready to roll!" I shouted.

"Mr. Richard. We are ready for your instruction." said Mahdi.

"Line everything up and fill them with fuel, including my vehicle, and bring me a list of the equipment."

"Yes sir."

The workers began immediately, preparing their equipment. Each dressed in long white clothes, with long knives protruding underneath their arms. Mahdi brings me a list and I began to place everything in a convoy. The workers were running to get underway. I liked the positive response I was receiving from the crew. Everyone was smiling as we prepared to move out.

"Mr. Richard. I will be your driver." said Mahdi.

"Great! I definitely need one after last night."

3

LAND OF DEARTH

The long line of equipment is over a quarter mile in length. I decided to return to the wadi I had crossed the night before. The souk trucks loaded with grain must be delivered before the grain rots. We'll arrive in a couple of hours and have a full day of road building. Traveling the small narrow camel trail, we arrive at the wadi at mid-morning. The souk trucks are still stranded on the opposite shore, waiting for the water to recede.

"Unload everything and put the large D-8 dozers out front!" I shouted.

Within 15 minutes the road building began with large boulders being removed with the huge dozers. The giant G-14 graders began to shape the terrain following close behind. The 966-loaders and tipper trucks were in full pursuit to stay up. I locate several areas of excellent material to be placed in the road. Over a dozen large tipper trucks began to haul the material as the souk truck drivers watched from the opposite shore. These workers have me convinced they have the experience to do the job. I have an immense feeling of joy deep inside, as I see the first mile of road being completed.

"Mahdi, return to the wadi and tell the souk drivers to cross now. If they get stuck, we will pull them out."

"O.K."

He shouted to the drivers and within minutes the trucks are in the water. I watch as each one pulls along side of us. They begin to follow close behind as we are en-route to the village of Gyaga, Sudan. The large earth moving equipment is pushing everything ahead, and we will be in the village with the food before dark.

This area is extremely dry, and dusty with the roughest terrain I've seen. Around 10 A.M. the heat is almost unbearable, and the sun is incredibly bright. I find no water for miles as we push through this forsaken land. It's hard to believe that any human being can survive under such harsh conditions. The Sudanese, and their Chadian counter-parts, are a resilient people. I had trained in the Mohave Desert and faced nothing as bone dead as Western Darfur. Giant termite mounds, and ant hills over 8 feet in height, are being pushed by the dozers. Millions of ants have covered the road just ahead. The dead foliage governs the area with nothing visibly green.

Many carcasses of animals litter the area from lack of food and water. The stench of death covers the area as we pass through a hoard of expired camels. Starving kids, with other family members, appear and begin to follow the con-

33

voy. They run behind the trucks knowing food is aboard. Barefoot, with little clothing, they endure the most extreme conditions to survive. They appear as mere skeletons with protruding eyes. Their small frame barely able to support them, as the skin has sank into their tiny faces. Yet they run with a smile upon their face as we enter the village. They have followed us for miles on foot to receive the grain. Sorghum and millet is the basic food supply on board the trucks.

The villagers are running to meet us we push into the city. We drive to the front of the convoy to meet the village Shak [shake] or leader. A frail man with open arms, greets us with a friendly smile, as he barely supports his frail body. The souk drivers are throwing the food to the villagers. The people scramble for every morsel of grain as it hits the ground.

"Mr. Richard, the Shak insist you drink tea with him." said Mahdi.

"Tell him I would be honored." I replied.

A small women appears and places a pot of water on an open campfire. Within minutes the boiling water is poured into a small cup. The Shak presents me with the steaming hot tea as we toast the arrival of the food. The small children would run up, grab a glimpse, and quickly disappear.

"They have never seen a Quawazi, or white-man before." said Mahdi.

"Tell the Shak we're here to help his people."

"He wants to show you something." said Mahdi.

"Sure." I replied.

We walk toward a rugged hillside, stopping at the base. The ground is covered with small boulders spread over a large area. They appear to be placed by hand. Each one has been

34

placed in a straight line.

"What is this?" I asked.

"Graveyard. The Shak said these are his villagers that have starved to death in the past 6 months."

"Tell him I'm sorry, and the food will continue to pass this way."

We turn and walk back into the village. The trucks have been emptied of all food. Everyone appears very happy as they begin preparing the food. None of them could have possibly been any happier than I. It's a wonderful feeling of accomplishment. I want to do more and decide to sit down with the drivers with a new plan.

"Tell the drivers to return to Nyala and continue to bring as much food as possible when it arrives."

Mahdi, tells them in Arabic and each driver nods his head in agreement.

"They want to know where the next shipment is going?" said Mahdi.

"Murnei." I replied.

"They agree. They will leave immediately."

"Mahdi, take the equipment and men just beyond the village and set up camp."

"O.K."

The men circle the camp with the equipment and hurriedly erect my tent. I will map out the area and have a plan in place for tomorrow. Several small villages are en-route to the main town of Murnei. I will place the road, so regular food shipments will pass through each village.

Darkness starts to surround us and a "Gra-furah" [Arabic for guard] is placed at my front door, as a goodwill gesture by the village Shak. I'm very happy to have witnessed the events that took place today. Every red blooded American would have gladly changed places with me. I can hardly wait until daylight, so we can begin another operation toward the next village. It'll be several days before another food shipment arrives in this area. We'll cover as much terrain as possible before they return.

A small boy arrives at my tent with 2 mangoes sent by the villagers. I'm thankful for them because I must live off the land, the same as my workers. Water is transported into the camp on the backs of local women. We fill every container available so we can survive until we reach the next village.

Daylight is approaching as I walk outside, seeing the workers asleep under their equipment. They're a tough group of individuals. The average wage is 30 dollars a month and no extras. No complaints, as they seem as eager as I to get the food shipments through. One by one, they start to rise with their prayer mats. Washing their hands and feet, they crawl onto the mats, and begin praying. I notice only one worker not praying. I stroll over and ask Mahdi why he isn't praying.

"I'm not Muslim." he said.

"What religion are you?" I asked.

"I'm nothing." He said.

"When the men finish praying have them mount up. We're going to the village of Sili today."

"No problem."

Each worker walks toward me smiling, saying warm greetings in Arabic. Each one begins fueling their equipment from the large fuel tanker. I appoint a mechanic to maintain my land rover and stay with me at all times. Within minutes we are ready to begin the day.

"Tell them we will take the lead, and follow as close behind as possible."

Mahdi tells the workers in their native tongue and they shake their heads in agreement. Within minutes we are pushing the giant rocks and ungodly terrain in a northwestern direction. I have the mechanic, guard and driver with me so we can scout ahead. We travel several miles without seeing any sign of life. Suddenly, a tire is beginning to go flat. The mechanic and guard jack up the vehicle. They remove the tire and begin to break it down by hand. They hammer away in the hot sunlight and begin to patch the tire. Taking a small air pump they fill the tire and we are on our way.

We arrive at a small wadi with no water present. Two young girls, digging in the center of the wadi, look for drinking water.

"Ask them where the village of Sili is located?"

"They say it is beyond those hills."

"Let's go."

We drive past a herd of camels being watered by a group of children. Large boulders surround the village making it almost impossible to enter. Stopping approximately 100 meters from the village we walk into a small group of grass huts. Inside we see starving men and women sitting with their frail bodies on the ground. Almost dead from starvation, they sit motionless, without expression. The flies are almost unbearable, as the heat is blistering down upon these poor souls. No one was stirring about the village as we walked into a small souk with only a few empty baskets.

"A very old man emerges from his hut and walks slowly

toward us."

"This is the village Shak." said Mahdi.

"Tell him what we are doing."

Mahdi begins speaking to the old man and he takes my hand with tears in his eyes. I had to look away before I lost control of my own emotions. I wave to the mechanic and guard to come with us. They ran up as we began to walk through the village and witness the horror. The villagers, sick and exhausted from the famine, appeared to weak to bury their dead.

"Tell the mechanic and guard to stay behind and bury their dead."

"O.K." said Mahdi.

"Tell them we will return in 2 days time."

"I will tell them."

We leave the small village and stop at the water hole with the camels and begin to fill our water can. The small frail bodies hold out their hands for food. I regretfully, have none to offer. We leave and head toward the equipment at full speed. We arrive at mid afternoon and continue to work until dark. We have a few mangoes and guavas and retire for the night.

I became very restless as I thought about the starving men, women, and children in Sili. I decide to light a candle and try to figure how to get the food deliveries faster. Almost 2 hours pass and I can't find a faster approach to the village. I put out the candle and try to get some rest. I am awakened, a short time later, by something moving inside the tent. I lay very still thinking, maybe I'm dreaming. A very soft scratching noise is directly over-head. I take the flash light and shine toward the roof of the tent. Crawling on the inside are hundreds of large, tarantula size spiders. Gray, hairy bodies are running all over the place. I ran outside, fleeing for my life. The guard ran inside and began to beat them with a club.

"What is wrong?" asked Mahdi.

"Huge spiders!" I said.

"Make sure you don't burn the candles after dark. The spiders are attracted to the light."

"I won't make that mistake again"

The guard assures me they're all gone. I walk back inside and wrap a large blanket around my entire body. I'm much to nervous to sleep, so I decide to stay outside in the land rover until morning.

After morning prayers, we are underway once again. We began the road at 6 A.M. sharp, hoping to make the village before dark. The equipment and operators are at full speed. I've never witnessed a better road crew. I'm very pleased with the progress being made.

The workers have proven they are equally concerned about the welfare of their fellow countrymen. The long treacherous hours in this barren land are beginning to pay off as we enter the village after dark. To tired to set up camp, everyone sleeps on the ground.

At daylight, I walk through the small village of Sili. The poor villagers are lying on small mats with little or no food. Very quietly, I roam through the streets which houses a stench of death in the air. I find my mechanic and guard sleeping under an open grass hut. I wake them and we move toward the equipment.

"I want you to begin fueling the equipment so we can move out." I said.

They nod their head in agreement and begin immediately. Tomorrow is Friday, a no-work day in the Muslim world. We'll press toward Talulu in an attempt to reach her tonight. The workers begin to stir about with their prayer mats. Mahdi approaches me, asking for instructions.

"We will move out at 6.A.M sharp."

"They will be ready."

"Tell the village Shak a food shipment will be through here in a couple days."

"O.K."

Looking toward the hillside I see a number of new rocks used as tombstones. The dearth is taking its toil in Western Darfur. The dreams of excitement and a new challenge in Africa were being met. This is by far the greatest challenge I have ever faced.

The daily rigors and harsh conditions make me rely on a Higher Power. The immense responsibility of deciding which village gets food next becomes nerve wrecking.

We are several miles from Sili, and encounter a large caravan of Chadian refugees. They're in search of food and try to stop the equipment.

"Tell them to follow the road to Sili. Explain to them food is in en-route."

"I'll tell them." said Mahdi.

I notice a woman riding a large Brahma bull. Others are walking and dragging everything they own. The men are all riding camels or Arabian horses. Most of the women are walking, many carrying small infants. Their frail bodies are a testament that the famine has spread into neighboring Chad. The sad little faces have a look of hope when told about the food en-route.

The long dusty road is taking shape as we scout ahead. The terrain shows no life as we endure the high temperatures reaching above 100 degrees. Water, more valuable than gold, is our only lifeline. We have no choice, but to continue to the village for supply of this precious commodity.

We finally arrive at the tiny village of Tululu. We are greeted by the locals as we prepare to set up camp. Many children stare as we unload our meager belongings. Tomorrow is Friday so I'll return to Nyala for further orders.

As daylight approaches, I refuel the land rover for the long trip. I wake Mahdi and we're gone in less than a half hour. We pass through the same villages we had left days earlier. We arrive at the wadi that previously flooded only to find a dry creek bed. Rounding a sharp curve, we encounter a shipment of grain aboard 6 souk trucks heading toward Sili and Tululu. A feeling of relief that those poor souls would live another day.

Arriving in Nyala, we find a member of the press from a prominent East coast newspaper. I'm warned to avoid him like the plague. I remember how the press hurt our troops in Vietnam, so I wasn't going to turn this into a charade. We enter the small office and pick up the orders to continue to Murnei. I have a new set of tires placed on the land rover and prepare to leave.

I am approached by two members of the press but manage to escape. I am only concerned about starving people, nothing else. I finally manage to find Ronnie before leaving the compound.

"What about a field radio?" I asked.

"Sorry, but you won't be getting one any time soon." said Ronnie.

"Murnei is still weeks away, so I can't say when I'll return."

"Just report back as soon as you reach Murnei. It's getting very close to the rainy season, so cover as much terrain as possible."

"O.K."

Passing through the tiny villages, children run with smiling faces, waving. It's a great feeling that cannot be described knowing just days earlier they faced certain death. This is only the beginning of a long treacherous journey into the unknown. Many more people are only days from starvation as time is quickly running out. Arriving in Tululu, we find the grain shipment has been dispersed among the people.

"Where are we going tomorrow?" asked Mahdi.

"We will head due west toward the village of Sauria. We will scout ahead of the equipment, marking the road. Tell the mechanic and guard to be prepared to move out at daylight."

"O.K."

The equipment begins to move at daylight, pushing due west. We're en-route early to avoid the high temperatures that are merciless. Around 10A.M. we pass a small valley surrounded by several large stones.

Inside we see several huts with camel skins wrapped around the top.

"Stop Mahdi. Let's go over and ask how far to the village

of Sauria."

We stop the land rover and stroll over to the small encampment. Walking to within 50 feet of the first small hut a doorway is opened. Suddenly a man emerges with a large knife and approaches us. I notice his throat has a large opening and his body is covered with sores. He tried to speak in a language Mahdi couldn't understand. He raised the long bladed knife over his head as we ran toward the land rover. We quickly left the area and continued toward the village, hoping they would be more receptive.

The terrain becomes very rugged and almost impassable. After several attempts to cross a hilly area, we are forced to go several miles around to reach the village. Arriving, we meet the village Shak, informing him we'll return within a couple days. We must leave in hopes of finding the equipment before dark.

We return and find the workers setting up camp approximately halfway to the village.

The following morning we are once again pushing due west toward Sauria. I have warned the workers not to stop near the small encampment in the valley. I can't afford to lose a single worker at this stage. We arrive at Sauria in mid-afternoon and set up camp. The entire village came to help us erect the army tent, and brought mangoes. Nothing else seems to grow in this area, as all crops lie dormant in the fields. The villagers know the road into the village means food is en-route.

We will service the equipment over the next two days. The harsh conditions have taken its toil on the blades of the graders. The tracks of the dozers will need to be adjusted and air filters changed. A fuel tanker is en-route because we are running dangerously low.

There are no complaints from the workers from the long hours. They equally understand the urgency of the hour. I map out the next stage of the operation. It will take several days to reach the wadi. I will place an order for several hundred Gabian baskets and build a bridge out of stones. These 1x2x3 meter baskets will be hand filled with stones and placed in the wadi. At flood stage they can be crossed with delineating post as guides. If the post aren't visible it will be too dangerous to cross.

I send several tipper trucks to Nyala to pick them up and return as soon as possible. The following morning several souk trucks arrive with the grain. The villagers climb aboard the trucks and remove the food in record time. No amount of money could buy what I was feeling. I look at the sacks of food, with the American flag draping the sides. I soon forget about my hunger pains as I walk through the masses of starving people. Each one is making bread and eating the Sorghum in the form of paste. This is the same grain we feed cattle in America, yet this is a delicate mix in Western Sudan.

4
A BRIDGE TOO FAR

We turn northwest today, towards Murnei. It's the largest village in the area where large groups of starving villagers have gathered. It will take several days to reach the area and we'll not rest until we reach her. The workers have started early and we're out front marking the route.

The long days began to pass very quickly, with little time to think of the outside world. This remote area is like going back in time thousands of years. Nothing present reminds one that we are in the 20th century. We're surrounded by open desert, littered with the carcasses of both man and beast. No sign of life can be seen in any direction. Our water, running dangerously low, is a reminder we must reach the village no later than tomorrow. We work late into the night once again, in an effort to achieve our goal.

The following morning we are desperate to push into

Murnei. I have Mahdi stress to the workers our present condition. They have assured me they will arrive before nightfall. We work with sheer determination not to stop before reaching the village. The long, dusty road is taking shape so food deliveries will reach this remote outpost.

As the sun begins to set a small glimpse of Murnei comes into view. We're out of water and hurriedly race towards the dry wadi. Women dip water into clay pots and walk towards the village. We have gone several hours without a single drop as we fall upon our faces and lap from the creek bed. My dry blistered lips have cracked under the extreme heat. Weakened by lack of food and dehydration, I have little strength left to enter the village. I crawl beneath my land-rover and settle in for the night.

The following morning we enter the village, finding many refugees from the surrounding area. All are suffering from malnutrition, many to weak to stand. We meet the village Shak who informs us many more are en-route and there is no food available.

"Tell him we should have a food convoy arriving soon."

Mahdi speaks briefly to the Shak, and he shows signs of joy as he turns to his people and conveys the message. A small crowd of people, barely standing, began to gather all around.

"He ask for you to dig out a large hole near the wadi, as a watering hole for the people."

"Tell him we will begin immediately."

The 2 large D-8 dozers pushed two huge craters near the village. We began pushing stones into piles so we could begin building one of the largest Gabian basket bridges in the world. It will take every able body in the village to assist in this endeavor. We cannot start until the villagers have received the food. We'll wait until the souk trucks arrive with food. The large tipper trucks should arrive tomorrow with the wire baskets for the bridge. We set up camp near the wadi and wait for the trucks. It will take approximately a week to build the bridge so the trucks can delivery food during the approaching flood season. The floods come very quickly and destroy everything in their path. The people cannot endure much longer without regular food deliveries.

The following morning the sound of trucks can be heard in the distance. The dust steady rises as they approach the village. The villagers swarm the dozen trucks of grain and empty them within the hour. The tipper trucks, loaded with Gabian baskets, have also arrived. The crew began to unload them at record speed.

"Ronnie sent you this paperwork." said Mahdi.

I return to my tent to go over the paperwork. A large stack of time sheets, along with a number of orders from Khartoum is enclosed. Another large envelope sealed with heavy tape accompanied the mail. Opening the letter, I see the bold letters saying, " THE NEWS REPORTER IS EN-ROUTE BY ANY MEANS POSSIBLE. TRY AND STAY AWAY FROM HIM. HE'S BAD NEWS!"

I've got roads and bridges to build so people enslaved by famine can be fed. I don't have time for interviews or photos. I write a letter and send it with the return vehicle letting Ronnie know, I'm not stopping the project. We will stay until the last soul is fed. I return to the village with Mahdi, finding the Shak dividing the food shipment. Large numbers of people have assembled for the sorghum. Waiting for the last of the food to be given out, we finally manage to speak with him.

"Tell him I need every man, woman, and child available tomorrow morning."

"He said he will send people into the surrounding area and have everyone at the wadi tomorrow morning."

"Tell him, I'll have Sudanese pounds sent from Nyala with the next shipment, and they'll be paid for their work."

"I have told him and he will have the village present tomorrow."

Night begins to fall in this remote region of Western Darfur. I take time to read my King James Bible, asking God for strength and guidance. It has been several weeks since I had a moment to myself. I was physically and spiritually exhausted. Suddenly, a voice rings outside my tent. Mahdi enters and ask about tomorrow. He looks at the Bible and asked, "How did you get this into the country?"

"The police at the airport picked it up a couple of times, without saying anything."

"They usually arrest everyone that's a Christian and take their bible." he said.

"I still believe in miracles." I answered.

"I also believe in them."

"Why aren't you Muslim, like all the others?"

"I was a devout Muslim for many years. A few years ago during Ramadan, [a forty day fast for Muslims] I decided to fast day and night. The average Muslim, fasts during the daylight hours, but eats during the night. I ate nothing 40-days, and 40-nights. My only prayer was for God to show me a vision of Mohammad."

"I said I would not eat until I had this vision. Very near the end of Ramadan, I saw a vision of a man burning in a hot fiery furnace. A voice spoke to me saying "Here is your Mohammed." I was very afraid, knowing I was serving a pagan god, burning in hell. I've never been a Muslim since." he said.

"You haven't tried another religion?"

"No, I really cannot. If I become anything other than Muslim, they'll kill me."

"What will the workers think if they find out I'm Christian?"

"They like you very much and are willing to work for you. They say you work very hard, and see you're suffering the same as they are. You are the best Quawagi in the world to them. They respect you a lot." he said.

"I am humbled by their kind words. I don't want to disappoint them, but I'm afraid the rains are going to stop us completely. I think we're to late to save the masses of starving people. It will take an Act of God to feed them. This is a shoe-string operation with no spare parts. Let the crew know I'm not leaving until we have nothing left to offer the starving people of Darfur."

"What about the bridge?"

"The bridge must be built immediately. We'll begin construction tomorrow morning."

"Do we have enough material in the area for the job?" asked Mahdi.

"Yes, just beyond that first small rise is a large deposit of stones. I want 20 tipper trucks and two 966 loaders positioned there in the morning. Place the G-14 graders in the wadi, at the crossing, leveling it straight across. Place 6 workers, as instructors on the Gabian baskets, to teach the villagers. Place the stones across the wadi in piles so the people will have access to them. The dozers will excavate the materials, beginning at daylight."

"How long will it take to complete?"

"If the Shak has a good turnout, it'll take approximately a week."

"I'll have the crew ready."

I was awakened at daylight, by the sound of many voices. The villagers had begun to assemble. Looking towards the wadi I see a large crowd of Sudanese, beyond all my expectations. At least 2,000 people have gathered to help with the bridge construction. The Shak had sent runners into the surrounding hillside and many had responded to the call. The endeavor to build the largest Gabian basket bridge in Darfur is underway.

The workers are non-stop through the grueling heat of the day. Everyone is working in unison as the villagers perform their assigned task. The small kids running with stones the size of baseballs as they are hand placed into the baskets. The long lines, resembling a chain-gang, toiled late into the evening hours. I send the word down the line to stop for the day. I'm amazed at the progress made today.

"There is an abundance of materials to complete the bridge." said Mahdi.

"Yes, only if we can have it in place before the first large flood. I am very pleased with the crew and villagers today. Please tell them I'm very pleased, and we'll begin again tomorrow."

A young kid runs to my doorway, leaving a piece of bread and 2 mangoes. It is a present, showing the appreciation of the local people. I'm honored to be in a position to help the villagers of Murnei.

The following morning, the number of workers has increased. Approximately 500 additional workers have engaged in the endeavor to complete the bridge. The new workers are refugees from the bordering nation of Chad. Sudan borders 9-separate countries with refugees from each nation.

I begin installing delineating post at each end of the bridge. They will warn the drivers during the floods if it's to dangerous to cross. The rains usually arrive from June to September in the amount of approximately 80 inches. The floods are devastating to the village people. Their crops can be gone in minutes by these deadly floods, originating in the hills. They appear much like a tidal wave with extreme force, leaving the villagers stranded for days.

The workers have completed the second day of the bridge. I am very pleased with the effort put forth today. I'm sure we can complete the bridge, at this rate, in a weeks time. I go over the final plans once more, to finish the job. A convoy has arrived from Nyala with more food, for the additional refugees.

A driver appears at my tent with additional orders and paperwork. Opening a double-taped letter from Ronnie, it reads, "BETTER HURRY-RAINS ON THE WAY." I can't work any faster or push the people any harder. They have gone beyond my expectations, especially being undernourished. I will continue with the bridge at first light.

I find the entire village at the wadi at daylight. Without

any supervision they have begun the treacherous job once again. All day long they toil in the unbearable heat, without breaks, to finish this lifeline to the outside world. They know this is their only hope during the floods to receive food via souk trucks.

A cry rings out at the center of the bridge. A small child has a compound fracture from the tremendous weight of a section of bridge. Several workers run to free the child as the weight has been lifted.

"Place him into the rear of my land-rover."

"The family ask for your help." said Mahdi.

"Tell them I'll do all I can."

I've only had a few classes of first aid training from the marine corp. I've never attempted this but I won't back out now. I stabilize the boy, and stop the bleeding with direct pressure. Placing a tight bandage over the wound I manage to re-set the bone. Amid the loud screams, two workers hold him tightly, as I apply the splints. I secure them above and below the nasty break. I have him carried to his small hut, along with his mother. The jubilant villagers, smile as they continue to build the bridge.

As darkness approaches the workers return to their grass huts. I decide to sit down in the large mud-hole, dug by the dozers. It is the first bath I've had since arriving 2 weeks earlier. I never would've dreamed, a month ago, I would be in this situation. I hadn't taken time to sit down and think about all that was happening in the world. I wish I had brought a short-wave radio to listen to the BBC. As the darkness surrounds me, I decide to return to my tent. I find Mahdi at the door, awaiting my return.

"The people really appreciate what you did today with the broken leg." he said.

"Tell them it was the least I could do. I'm very sorry this happened. We'll keep a closer eye upon the villagers tomorrow."

"The mother said he's resting fine."

"I will check on him again tomorrow. I got a message today the rain is on the way. I don't want to push the workers. We'll work as long as possible each day. If the rains come we will work between the flooding."

"The workers said they will work day and night if you ask them."

"Tell the workers I'm very pleased with each of them. The working hours will remain the same."

The following morning the count of workers has increased to around 3,000. Word has gotten to the surrounding areas about the food deliveries. The Shak tells them when they arrive they must work on the bridge for food. I like his new concept to obtain new workers. I decide to place a sign in English and Arabic over the bridge saying, "WILL WORK FOR FOOD."

I walk down a long stretch of finished bridge. The villagers continue smiling, as they do back breaking work. Never a complaint as they refuse to stop during the long daylight hours. We are past the halfway mark. If the rains can hold off 2 more days, we will be able to cross the wadi above flood stage.

The darkness arrives once again as the workers head toward their small grass huts. We are over 60% complete with the largest Gabian basket bridge in Sudan. It is a feat I didn't believe possible, because of the immense heat and lack of manpower. The sheer idea this could be achieved was mind boggling. I'm getting very anxious to see the completion of the bridge. It's getting even more difficult to sleep, as I lie awake, worrying about the rainy season.

Day four, at this remote location, has a large turnout once again. The large crowd has became faster and more efficient in their work. I can hardly believe the motivation of these people in great peril. Famine is prevalent among all of the villagers. Most have lost loved ones, yet they toil in the blistery, hot sun without complaint.

Suddenly, and without warning, a dark cloud begins to loom on the horizon. The workers continue to toil on the bridge. The wind began to blow very hard, as sand plummeted against us.

"Tell the workers to secure the area and go home."

"O.K." said Mahdi.

A large sandstorm intermingled with heavy rain begins to fall. Everyone is running toward shelter as the first deluge of the rainy season finally arrives. Our work comes to a halt as we wait out the deadly storm.

The rain is falling so hard I must place a new support to keep the tent from falling. The water runs inside at a rapid rate. I climb on top of a small cot to wait out the flood. The heavy rain increased in volume with each passing minute.

The wadi begins to climb above flood stage very rapidly. We were so close to completion of the bridge. I see the water rising above the bridge and start to erode the open areas not yet completed. Several of the empty wire baskets begin to tumble, as the high water washes them from sight.

All the hard work is on the verge of being completely destroyed. What will I tell the villagers if we lose the bridge? The floods are destructive, because the river bed is shallow. This allows the flood waters to run on top of the ground. Nothing can stand against the flood waters once they have covered the delineating post. The rushing of the water coming from the hills sounds like a train approaching.

The entire night we are inundated with heavy flooding. Higher and higher the water rises, as the rain pounds the small village of Murnei. The following morning the rain begins to subside, as a ray of hope begins to shine. I walk toward the wadi, not knowing what to expect. Surprisingly, the bridge only suffered minimal damage. Looking behind, I see Mahdi running towards me.

"Did the bridge hold?" he shouted.

"Yes! Thank you Jesus!" I shouted.

"Thank you Jesus!" he shouted back.

"I want the grader operators to ditch this entire area."

"I will get them now."

I have no idea how long it will be before the next flooding will occur. Only that I will do everything I possibly can to finish the bridge.

After an hours time, the graders have diverted a tremendous amount of water. The water falls below the delineating post exposing a large amount of washed out areas.

Several dozen Gabian wire baskets are missing, possibly buried beneath the sand. The large holes in the wadi will be repaired, and we will start anew.

"Tell the Shak to fall the villagers out and we will work until the rains return."

"He said he will be prepared for your orders. I will have them report to the bridge."

Standing in knee deep water the villagers began to sift through the stones. Taking the wire baskets, work resumes once again. The graders and loaders operate at full speed to reshape the terrain. Leveling the interior area to fit the wire baskets, filled to capacity.

Surprisingly, a large number of villagers from the surrounding areas are appearing to resume work. The numbers steadily increase, as we neared completion. Only a miracle will allow us time to finish before the rainy seasons takes control of the entire operation.

"The sky is turning dark again." said Mahdi.

"We will have to work in between the storms. They will increase in regularity until it is nonstop for the entire season."

"What will we do if we don't finish the bridge?" asked Mahdi.

"Then the village will be cut of from further food shipments."

"The Shak says he is nearly out of food once again, because of the large influx of refugees."

"Tell him I understand his concern. We will do everything in our power to see his village isn't cut off."

The workers are at full speed as they fight against the elements. The soggy mud bottom wadi, along with the tremendous winds, blowing the oncoming storm directly toward us. The sky turns dark once again, as the rains starts to fall. Heavy sheets of water plummet the ground, as the villagers once again flee into their huts.

Rapidly, the wadi is full above capacity, as the rising water drenches the land of Darfur. The rains have increased in velocity as it takes a toil on the bridge once again. There is nothing we can do but wait and pray.

The hours passed very slowly as I find myself alone, in a flooded tent, halfway around the world. Nothing but a handful of mangoes and guava for food. No outside communication, as I sit stranded in a strange land. I find my clothes starting to sag from weight loss.

What I would give to have a conversation with another American. I'm getting physically weak as I begin to have hunger pains. I will read the only book I have available, the King James Bible. I began to find added strength, as the hours turned into days, and the rain doesn't let up. I begin to read about Jesus alone in a desert place. [Mark chapter-6]. I began to feel relief from the burden of being alone in the desert. I've been confined to the tent for 3 days without a break in the rain. The water has completely shut the operation down. Mahdi enters the tent for the first time since the rain began.

"The Shak says the village is nearly out of food. He wants to know when another shipment might arrive."

"Tell him there's nothing I can do now. We'll all have to wait until the rain stops again and see if anything arrives."

"The entire village knows you have done your very best. The construction crew say they can't believe the effort you're putting forth to help a people you don't even know."

"Tell them we're not going anywhere until this bridge is completed."

"I'm glad your here with us Mr. Richard. You have given all of us hope."

"Thanks for the kind words. We'll all feel better when the rain stops."

The rain started to slow during the night time hours. As daylight approaches, only a small drizzle remained. I walk toward the wadi, only seeing the dangerous water rushing through the area, covering the bridge. It will be a miracle if any of the bridge is remaining as this giant tidal wave shows no mercy. It will take another day for the water to drop below flood stage, so work can resume. All day long, I sit and pray for the water to fall, before another flood appears.

The following morning the water began falling below flood stage. The top of the bridge was barely visible as we watched from shore. As the noon hour approached, I give the word to resume work.

The villagers gracefully took their place and try once again to beat the elements. Only minor damage was found and quickly repaired. Standing in knee deep water, the villagers toiled into the evening hours.

"The bridge is very near completion. If the weather holds it should be completed tomorrow."

"I will tell the workers to work even faster tomorrow." said Mahdi.

The workers and villagers gather together to share their food. I see joy in the faces of everyone as they realize the nearness of the completion of the bridge. After breaking bread with the villagers, I retire to my quarters. I am proud of the dedication of the Sudanese people. They are a determined people who have a will to resist the worst of conditions, and overcome defeat. They have been an inspiration to me in their will to survive. Sleep escapes me, as I imagine the final section of the bridge being placed.

The final day of bridge building has arrived, as the entire village gathers at the wadi. Working in unison, everyone is in a race against time. The sun is slightly covered from the dark clouds, as a storm appears once again on the horizon.

Hour after hour, they toil in the heat as they refuse to stop. We are threatened by the severe weather that continues to defy us. The rain begins to fall as the villagers resist and continue working. The swollen water continues to rise, as the villagers continue to fill baskets. We're within reach of our goal as the last few baskets are placed. The workers refuse to stop, and will soon be cut off from the village, as the dangerous water continues to rise.

"Tell them to run to the village now!" I shouted.

Several hundred villagers begin to flee for their lives, running down the center of the bridge. The waters start to creep above the wire baskets as the rains increase in velocity. The workers cheer from the opposite shore of the wadi, as the last section of the bridge is placed. The waters have cut them off from the village, as they stubbornly fought the elements in completing the bridge. A loud sound of jubilation can be heard from the singing villagers, on a job well done.

The dangerous waters have once again appeared as each of us breathed a sigh of relief. The workers stranded on the opposite shore will have to wait for the rising water to fall. A small sacrifice, by these brave people, in an attempt to save their village from certain starvation. I am very proud to have been a small part in the completion of this bridge. The people of Sudan have given me encouragement to continue in the operation.

The night hours bring a small celebration among the villagers. They gather to celebrate the completion of the bridge. Only a small amount of food remains as they share the last morsel among themselves.

After falling asleep, I'm awakened by a sound of someone being beaten. A loud bop-bop sound with moaning can be heard, outside the tent. Rising, with flashlight in hand, I proceed to investigate the beating sound. Shining atop the fuel tanker a man is standing with a long rope in hand. I walk over and see several men on the opposite side, with long poles in their hands. A large dog, with a lasso around his neck, is stretched out and being beaten.

"What is going on here?"

"The workers are going to eat the dog in celebration of the bridge." said Mahdi.

"Why are they beating him?"

"They believe he has evil spirits, and they must beat them out before he can be eaten."

Suddenly a man rushes forward, cutting the dogs throat, and hangs him upside down. Then they proceed to skin him as they prepare the fire for roasting. After being barbecued, the workers stand in line to eat.

"Mr. Richard, eat, eat." they said in broken English.

"No thanks." I answered.

They begin to laugh as I decline once again, to share their meal. As daylight approaches the men sit chewing on the remainder of the bones. I begin to recollect that I haven't seen many dogs in Sudan.

The sound of trucks can be heard in the distance. We watch as the souk trucks begin to drive across the bridge with a welcoming cry from the villagers. A dozen trucks loaded with grain exit the bridge and arrive in the village of Murnei.

Our job is completed, as we prepare to leave this tiny village. We must proceed further into the famine ravished countryside. A driver approaches with new orders from Khartoum, via Nyala. Opening the letter it read, "Proceed to build road toward Zalingei and build new bridge across Wadi Azum." I'm not sure if time will permit the construction of another bridge, before the rainy season sets in. We'll proceed with caution and build a road in the direction of the infamous Wadi Azum.

"Tell the crew to prepare to mount up."

"Where are we going?" asked Mahdi.

"We're heading due east toward Zalingei."

"Isn't that in the opposite direction?"

"Yes. We're going to open a road from Murnei to Zalingei and attempt to build a bridge across Wadi Azum. Weather permitting, it would be longer than the one we built here."

"Do you think we can beat the rains?"

"No. I really think we'll be very fortunate to reach Zalingei before the floods arrive."

"I'll have the men to mount up now."

The large dozers are in the lead with the graders following closely as we leave the small village behind. The children run along side for about a half-mile waving goodbye. I will miss the faithful hardworking villagers of Murnei.

5

DARKNESS IN DAFUR

We're easily reminded of our direction, by the rising of the sun. Each morning the brightness is welcomed as the rainy season is delayed. Only a couple of sporadic showers the past 2 days out of Murnei. We have encountered several small caravans fleeing the harsh famine in Darfur. We manage to reach a small water hole in mid-afternoon, and decide to stay for the night. We fill everything that'll hold water, before we attempt crossing the treacherous barren area tomorrow. A caravan of Chadians is heading in our direction. A number of men, women, and children stop at the water hole deciding to camp for the night. They build a large camp fire and begin to cook a large portion of meat.

"What are they cooking, Mahdi?"

"They butchered a camel."

"Are you going to eat with them?"

"No, we aren't invited." he said.

"Do you guys have any food?"

"Yes, we packed in a couple of sacks of grain. It should last until Zalingei. What are you eating?"

"I've got 6 mangoes and a small sack of guavas." I answered.

As daylight approaches, we refuel all equipment and continue to push eastward. The Chadians began to follow close behind with their caravan. The heat begins taking its toil early, as the storm clouds began forming on the horizon.

We're nearing the small village of Deirirro, Sudan. The terrain is extremely difficult to maneuver around. We take the dozers, level a small hill, and use the materials to fill the ungodly craters. A twin engine aircraft flies over very quickly and darts off in the distant sky. I can't imagine who would be in this area. It must be someone lost and trying to find their way. We continue to push massive amounts of filler into the ravines. This will assist the souk trucks in delivering the food. Several hours have passed and 2 camels are approaching from the east. One of the riders is a white man. I recognized him as one of the top officials of Arkel-Talab. He leaps from the camel and begins cursing and swearing like a drunk sailor.

"What's wrong with you?" I ask.

"Didn't you get my note?" he screamed.

Immediately a dozen workers ran towards the man, thinking he was going to kill me. They had drawn their long knives in defense of me.

"It's O.K. Return to work." I said.

They stood for a minute watching the man and slowly returned to their equipment.

"What note are you talking about?" I asked.

"I threw out a piece of paper as we flew over, for you to follow us and pick me up." he said.

"I have no idea about what you're talking about. The note could have landed in Chad. You were doing about 200 mph. Besides, I'm trying to build the road before the floods set in for the season. If you would provide me with a radio, you wouldn't have to toss out notes." I said.

"I've got more orders for you. The entire project is in jeopardy, so you've have got to act fast. I want you to continue on to Zalingei. We have got hundreds of trucks awaiting the grain in Nyala. The train heading toward Nyala is loaded, but the tracks are almost gone. I want you to split your crew in half at Zalingei. Send half of them toward El Geniena, and the other half to build a half mile bridge in Zalingei."

"I've only got half as many men and equipment as needed for this operation now. The floods are only a couple days away at most. You send those men into the hills and they'll be stranded for months."

"I don't care about that now. We'll worry about that later. You continue on towards Zalingei and divide them upon arrival. Do you understand me?" he said.

"Yes sir!" I said.

"Now, drive me to my plane so I can return to Khartoum." he said.

Without saying another word, I drove him to the plane. He climbed aboard and was soon out of site. I return and continue the road building. We stop on the east side of the village of Deirirro, to camp for the night.

Mahdi enters my tent and asks, "What was that all about

today?"

"It's proof that you cannot build a road from a desk in Khartoum 600 miles away."

"What does he have in mind?" he asked.

"He wants to split the crew in half, sending them towards the hill country in the flood season."

"I can't believe anyone would make that foolish mistake." he said.

"Don't say anything about this to the crew. I believe if we're fortunate enough to make it to Zalingei, it will be a miracle."

"I agree. Those storm clouds are starting to appear more frequently."

"The train is in trouble between Khartoum and Nyala. The floods have washed away most of the tracks, and they're grabbing at straws to make everything work. Tell the men, we'll leave at first light."

"I'll have them ready."

The sun is darkened, once again, by the storm clouds as we push due east. The Chadian caravan continues to follow us. The equipment is working at full speed as we near the outskirts of Zalingei. We drive ahead and enter the small town of grass huts and primitive shelters. The village Shak appears and we drink tea together, as he tells us where to camp.

We place the equipment in a circle, similar to an old western wagon train. We walk to the largest wadi in Darfur, the notorious Wadi Azum. It appears to be at least a half-mile across at this junction. We'll begin immediately on shaping the terrain in preparation for the bridge.

"Place the dozers on that ridge and begin pushing the stones. Have the G-14s open the wadi 50 feet in width. Place every tipper truck along that ridge, with two loaders, and we'll work until dark."

"O.K." said Mahdi.

The villagers lined the wadi watching our every move. We cannot proceed beyond the excavation of the bridge until the arrival of additional Gabian baskets. As darkness arrives, the surface of the wadi is ready for construction.

As daylight appears, a convoy of trucks begin to enter the village. A dozen trucks of grain and several trucks of wire baskets have arrived. The villagers climb the sides of the vehicles, and very quickly unload their precious cargo. Within minutes, a land rover appears with 2 white men and a Sudanese driver. They walk straight toward me, carrying a briefcase.

"Are you the Field Supervisor for Arkel-Talab?" they asked.

"Yes." I answered.

"We need to talk in private."

Both men were heavy set, around fifty, with thinning hair. One appeared to be a body guard of Korean descent. The other, an American, was well dressed, educated with a precise vocabulary.

"Who are you?" I asked.

"I'm with a prominent east coast newspaper and I'm following up a lead." he said.

"What kind of lead would attract you to this land of desolation?"

"First, we would like to look through the shipment that has just arrived."

"Please, feel free to look about the area."

The two men walk through the large sacks of grain as the food is being distributed. They climb into the rear of each souk truck, and begin to take pictures. I was puzzled at the their behavior, as I stood and watched.

"What do they want?" asked Mahdi.

"I have no idea." I answered.

They look at every single item delivered by the trucks. A driver gives me a stack of paperwork from Nyala. I return to my tent reading the orders. Within minutes, the two men reappear.

"May we come in?" they ask.

"Sure, have a seat."

"I've been trailing your every move for the past month." said the reporter.

"Why would you do a thing like that?"

"We need to discuss what your doing out here." he said.

"Look, what you see is what you get. I've been building roads through a dozen villages. We built the Gabian bridge at Murnei. I've witnessed several food shipments arrive in half a dozen villages. We are currently in the process of building possibly the largest Gabian bridge in the world. I'm facing inclement weather, with little or no resources. We're at least 6 months behind, with limited equipment and personnel."

"Do you want to see what the newspapers are reporting?"

"Yes, I really would like to know."

"This one says, "FAMINE RELIEF EFFORT HAS BOGGED DOWN IN SUDAN." Another one reads,

"FARMERS DIE IN FIELDS AS RESULT OF FAILED

OPERATION."

"Do you know why your operation has been delayed 6 months?" he asked.

"No, I'd like to know." I said.

"You're only a pawn out here. I'm going to show you what's really going on. Here are the official documents signed by the president of Sudan, Jaffar Mohammed Nimeiri. It is a contract for Arkel-Talab to drag its feet in the famine relief. This gives the United States government time to build the roads in Western Darfur." he said.

"I don't follow what your saying." I said.

"The food deliveries are being made under the condition that the United States be allowed to bury nuclear waste in this remote desert region. Some of the trucks are using your roads to bury nuclear waste."

"What you're saying is almost unbelievable. I haven't seen anything but food and wire baskets."

"The nuclear waste was delayed, thus the food had to wait. Once the nuclear waste arrived, the food deliveries began. They are jumping through hoops now trying to get these roads built. If I were you I'd keep my eyes open for anything or anyone suspicious."

"The only thing I'm sure about is there's over 3.5 million starving refugees in Sudan, and thousands have died. I'm building the roads to get the food through. That's what I've been hired to do, and I'm not stopping this operation."

"Do you know who your working for?" he asked.

"No. I only know I'd do this for free to save these people from certain death."

"Your working for a spook company. This food operation

is only a store front. You have no idea what is going to happen when the nuclear waste begins to take its toil." he said.

"I haven't seen anything that resembles nuclear waste. I've only got your word against theirs. I will not stop the famine relief effort over a few accusations." I said.

"If I were you, I'd check every truck coming through, making sure it was food." he said.

"What do I do if I find trucks loaded with nuclear waste? I couldn't stop them if I wanted to."

"You can get into contact with me and we'll bust this story wide open." he said.

"Yes, like you reporters did to us in Vietnam, right."

"You were in Vietnam?" he asked.

"Yes. I remember the press was the real enemy. Now I don't know who to believe. I only know you should have had your camera in the last 3 villages as we helped bury their dead. No, you don't want to publish a story about hungry, sick, or dying children do you. You just want to attack Americans trying to do a humanitarian job for the United States."

"I've actually seen the mass graves your men dug. We have exhumed some of them making sure they were graves and not nuclear waste dumps." he said.

"You actually dug into some of the graves, checking for nuclear waste."

"I didn't do any digging. I had the villagers do it for me."

"What did the Shak of the villages have to say about you excavating their graves?"

"He didn't like it at all." he said, laughing.

"How did you persuade him into allowing you to dig up the graves?"

"I told him we would cut off his food deliveries if they tried to stop us."

"You are lower than a snakes belly, you scummy pig. If you don't get out of here I'm going to stomp your guts out!" I screamed.

They fled from the tent as several workers arrived. They jumped into their land rover and headed south. I'm sure they won't return anytime soon.

"What was that all about?" asked Mahdi.

"I'll tell you later. What about the bridge?"

"We've got every available man, women, and child filling the baskets. We finished a section but it's going to take more time than expected. We're having to haul the rocks much further than before." he said.

"What about the Chadians?" I asked.

"They refuse to work. The men say that is beneath them."

"Let's go see about that."

We walk towards the Chadians who have entered the village for food. The men are lying around as the women wait upon them like servants.

"Tell them to get on their feet and go to work on the bridge now!" I said.

Mahdi speaks to them as they continue to ignore us. They begin laughing and eating the grain.

"Go get both dozers!" I said.

"I'll get them now." said Mahdi.

Within minutes both large D-8 dozers were coming across the wadi and pulled up along side. They dropped their huge blades at the Chadians feet.

"Tell the Chadians to leave now!"

The laughing stops, as they mount their camels and head north into the hill country.

"Tell the dozer operators to return to work."

"Thanks Mr. Richard. The morale of the workers was dropping as they watched the Chadians refusal to work. Things will be better now." said Mahdi.

"We've got to throw everything we have into the bridge. The floods are on the way."

"The villagers are concerned about their chances of being cut off from the food."

"Tell them if that happens, we will be cut off together. We're not leaving them stranded here all alone."

A constant barrage of rolling thunder echo from the hills. The sky, blackened from the storm, brewing to our east. The workers continue to fill baskets as the bridge continues to take shape. We're on borrowed time as we face the cutting edge of the rainy season that arrives without mercy. The wind from a coming sand storm is blasting us with dust and sand. I can barely breath, as I lean into the gale force winds.

"Pass the word down the line to secure everything and get in the village." I shouted.

Mahdi ran down the long section of completed bridge, spreading the word. The villagers ran for cover as the storm pelted us with huge drops of rain and sand. I seek cover in the tent as the last worker enters the village. Within minutes, the sky is black as the deadly storm begins to rage in Darfur Province. The storms are increasing like birth pangs, each more violent and closer together than the previous one. Mahdi races to the tent covered with dust and sand, soaking wet from the heavy rain.

"We're almost out of time aren't we?" he asked.

"Yes. I want the equipment placed on higher ground when the storm passes. We'll prepare for the worst and pray for the best." I said.

"Mr. Richard. What did those 2 men want earlier today?"

"Mahdi, we need to go over a few things, so pull up a seat. Those guys were newspaper reporters from the United States. I'm not sure if I can believe the story I've been told. I have to admit things are running much later than scheduled for the relief. The plane that landed with the official 2 days ago, advised me to speed things up, while everyone in Khartoum is dragging their feet. The roads and bridges should have been built 6 months ago, not during the rainy season. I walked through the grain shipments while in Khartoum, and it was rotting on the ground. The guards posted said they were ordered not to move it."

"I don't understand what you're saying." he said.

"Look, I want you to know that the average American doesn't have a clue what's happening in our own government. We pay our taxes and do what we're told. Millions of American dollars are being sent to Sudan by tax payers to help your people. We don't want to harm your people at all. I want you to understand that before we continue."

"Our people believe America is good for us." he said.

"I want you to give me your word you will not repeat what I'm about to say."

"Mr. Richard. You're my friend, and I give you my word this will not be spoken again."

"O.K. I want every truck entering our area to be searched."

"What are we going to be looking for?"

"Nuclear waste." I answered.

"Why would they ship nuclear waste to starving people?"

"Few people, and lots of sand. They would prefer to hide it in a remote area like this. Nomadic people with no communications, or cameras."

"What will the containers look like?"

"Metal drums. It must be moved in metal containers." I answered.

"What will we do if we find them?"

"We will not bury nuclear waste on my watch!"

"What will we do with it?" he asked again.

"Just wait and see."

"We trust you with our life. I will do what you say."

"This is our secret. We'll continue with business as usual. We'll work on the road and bridge under a new watchful eye. Remember, we'll search every truck in our area starting today."

Water receding at Bridge in Murnei

Bridge under construction at Murnei

Young Sudanese girl gathers water

Women carry food upon head

Food supply trucks broken down

Rear wheels fall from beneath truck

Tipper truck broke down in Wadi Azum

Souk truck broke down in Wadi Azum

G-14 Road grader stuck in Wadi

Building road in rainy season

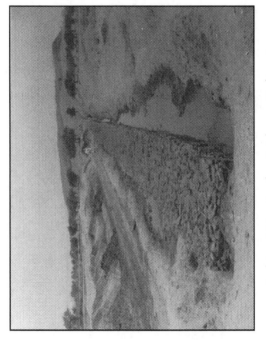

Gabian Wire Basket Bridge at Zalingei

Gabian Bridge over half mile in length

Sudanese woman on camel

Sudanese woman on Brahma bull

Giant ant hill (over 8 feet tall)

Camel caravan passing through Zalingei

Village near Tawila

Tan door oven at Tawila

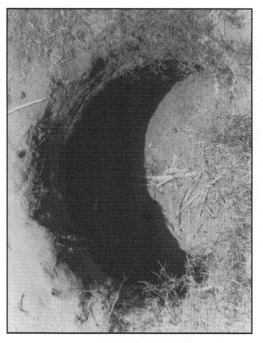

Dry water hole at Kebkabiya

Water hole at Kebkabiya

Sudanese women sift through dirt for grain

Women gather water for animals

Young girls gather firewood

Women do most of the work

Mahdi and myself on D8K dozer

My 1958 Land Rover under giant tree

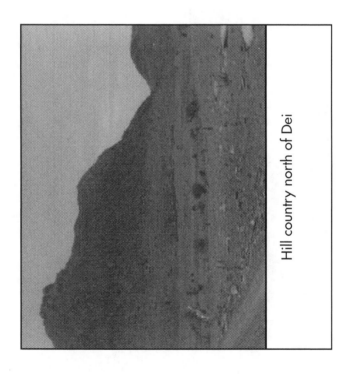

Hill country north of Dei

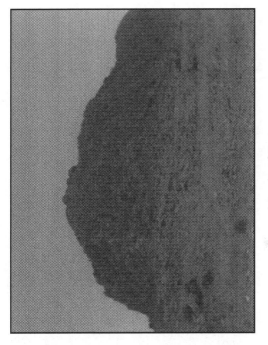

North of Dei

Hut near village of Dei

Village of Dei

Souk truck lost in Wadi Azum

Workers attempt to retrieve souk truck

Nayla, Sudan
Train from Khartoum overloaded with passengers

Nyala, Sudan - Grain loaded onto souk trucks

6
A DELUGE OF NEW TROUBLE

For several years the drought stricken people of Western Darfur prayed for rain. Today, that prayer is being answered by the tremendous storms that's unleashing its wrath across Wadi Azum. This long, dry river bed is being pounded by the flash floods in the area. This blessing can quickly turn into a curse as the starving millions of famine ravished people become cut off from food deliveries. Only a fraction of the food destined for this area has been delivered, and the remainder appears to be in jeopardy.

The storm continued to pound the village during the early morning hours. As the noon hour approaches the sound of souk trucks can be heard crossing the wadi. Suddenly, Mahdi appears in my tent.

"I am ready to begin searching the trucks." he said.

"Tell the villagers to stay put until we're through."

"I'll take care of it."

The trucks stop in the center of the village. We climb aboard the first 2 vehicles, loaded to capacity, and begin our search. We continue to search each truck, finding nothing out of the ordinary. I pass the word to begin unloading.

A driver brings me a stack of papers from Nyala. I return to my quarters and begin to file through the paperwork. Several memos from Khartoum accompanied the folder with warnings about the flooding.

The first one reads, "The torrential rains have washed out the railroad in 9 places. Food deliveries will be affected as the tracks become impassable. Over 500,000 tons of food is piled, ready for shipment. We fear 100,000 Sudanese will die in the next three months. Please continue to push through to the out lying areas as quickly as possible."

Opening a second memo it reads, "Less than a third of the starving people in Western Darfur is receiving food and medical supplies. Africa is being plagued by drought, famine, and now flooding. Our transportation is presently in a quagmire, as the roads and rail lines become impassable."

Another memo reads, "As the situation in Sudan deteriorates many foreign aid workers are beginning to leave. A lack of roads has kept food distribution rates well below the minimum needs of the famine stricken victims. A civil war is underway in the south as many Christians have been slaughtered. Please be advised that if it becomes necessary to flee the Western Darfur area, proceed to Central Africa."

I decide to read the letter from Ronnie in Nyala. He is the only one I feel I can trust at this point. Opening the tightly sealed envelope it reads, " Richard, you're fixing to be in a very precarious situation. Everything is falling apart as the floods begin racking havoc on the entire operation. I'm sorry, you're going to be stranded without food or radio communication for quite a while. I will try to send another convoy in your direction, but I can't guarantee its arrival. I warn you to be very careful of the typhoid and cholera outbreak in your area. Try to survive the best you can until the flood season is over. If possible try to return to Nyala! Cheers, Ronnie."

Even without the drought, flooding, or civil war Sudan would be in shambles. Every foreign effort to promote development has failed. It seems no cure is available for the current inherent ailment of Sudan. The very tools of survival have been threatened, as farmers eat the oxen used for plowing. They now rely on simple hand tools to scratch the furrows in the crust like soil.

The floods are now nonstop as the water continues to rise. There's nothing we can do, but wait out the rainy season. The swollen wadi now threatens the village, as it climbs above its banks. The long hours turn into days as we sit isolated from the world. Day after day, I sit alone in the desert with my King James Bible. It gives me hope in a land of sorrow and death.

Over a week has passed and the rain continues to fall. Only a small section of the bridge remains as the huge tidal waves continue to flow from the surrounding hills. The village of Zalingei takes a pounding as the soggy grass huts sway from the storm. The equipment sits atop the high ground as we await our fate.

Mahdi enters my tent for the first time in a week. Soaking wet, after wading in knee deep water to wrestle the drenching rain.

"It doesn't look good for the bridge." he said.

"We'll start over when the flood waters recede"

"Will you split the crew in half and send them north after the rain stops."

"No. We're going to stick together and do this right."

"What about the order to split up the crew."

"Look Mahdi. If their plan is to send nuclear waste mixed into the food shipments, they'll try to bypass us. They will follow the other unsuspecting crew and avoid us like the plague. They will have no choice but to follow us now."

"Your right, Mr. Richard. They wanted us to split so they could avoid us."

"Do you have any food left?" I asked.

"Yes, probably more than you." he said.

"I've got 2 mangoes left, that's it."

"We've got several bags of grain. I'll have some bread sent over tonight."

"Thanks Mahdi. Tell the crew we'll begin as soon as the rain stops."

"O.K. I'll tell them."

Another week of depressing rain falls in this remote region of Western Sudan. I've had plenty of down time, gathering my thoughts about the critical situation we find ourselves in. The lack of food and morale is at an all time low. There's absolutely nothing dry within several hundred miles. I'm beginning to feel like Noah as he sat in the Ark.

After a month of flooding the rain starts to subside. Finally, its safe to walk outside, without getting soaked. I look and see everyone coming out of their covey holes to walk around. Mahdi comes running with a jubilant smile.

"Thank you Jesus!" I shouted.

"Thank you Jesus! he shouted back.

"Tell the crew to begin starting their equipment. It's probably going to take a while to dry out."

"We'll get everything running." he said.

We spend the entire day drying everything, as we prepare to resume work. The water is entirely too deep to enter the wadi. We'll wait until tomorrow before attempting to move the equipment. As noon approaches, several souk trucks manage to reach the opposite side of the wadi. They stop and the drivers climb out, looking at the water level.

"I pray they don't try to cross now." said Mahdi.

"Tell them to stay put until tomorrow. The delineating post are underwater, warning us it's to dangerous."

Mahdi screams the command to stay put on the opposite side until tomorrow. The souk drivers continued to pace up and down the wadi for almost and hour. Suddenly, the engines are running and the trucks are starting to move.

"What are they doing?" I asked.

"Their probably going to back up and camp for the night." said Mahdi.

Suddenly, a large splash is heard and engines roaring. Three of the souk trucks enter the wadi, at full speed.

"Tell them to stop!" I shouted.

After a few seconds all three trucks were in trouble. The strong undercurrent capsized the trucks without mercy. The trucks rolled over several times, losing their precious cargo as the drivers leap from the trucks. Fighting for their lives, the current quickly swallowed each truck, along with their drivers. It was a foolish act that could have been prevented. If they had only stayed put, everything would have been saved. It was such a waste of human life and much needed supplies. The remainder of the trucks stayed on the opposite shores, choosing to avoid the same mistake made by their companions.

"I'm sorry, Mr. Richard. I told them to stay put until morning."

"You did your best Mahdi. We'll check the wadi in the morning and let the others know if it's safe to cross."

"What about the lost trucks?" he asked.

"We'll dig them from the bottom of the wadi and search them when the water recedes. If those trucks had nuclear waste onboard, we'd best be finding out and soon."

"Yes. I forgot about that. We'll dig them out as soon as these trucks leave." he said.

"As soon as these trucks cross over tomorrow we'll search them. Let the villagers distribute the food and we'll let the trucks return to Nyala. I want everything we have at the wadi tomorrow morning."

"O.K. We'll have everything ready."

The following morning the water level is safe to cross. We pass the word and the remainder of the souk trucks enter the water, arriving safely in the village. We climb aboard the trucks and find nothing suspicious. The village Shak begins to distribute the food as we place the equipment near the edge of the wadi. A driver brings me a stack of paperwork with additional orders. The trucks begin the long return trip, as we prepare to enter the water.

"Tell the workers to be very careful. I don't want to lose anyone."

"They'll be extremely careful, after the accident." said Mahdi.

The top of one of the washed away trucks is barely visible in the wadi. We fasten a large chain beneath, and begin to pull with a D-8 dozer. It will not move as we try in vain to salvage it from the murky water. We decide to wait a few hours until the flood water has completely dropped, leaving a dry creek bed once again. The chain suddenly snaps under the tremendous weight. We decide to dig everything from around the truck, and only search through the cargo aboard. Finding only wet soggy grain, we dig the second truck and find nothing out of the ordinary. The third truck cannot be found, only a section of the rear wheels lie exposed in the wadi bottom. Pushing large amounts of sand from the wadi finally exposes a small portion of the truck.

"The villagers say they will finish digging by hand." said Mahdi.

"Issue the shovels and we'll keep a close eye for anything suspicious."

Dozens of workers were digging non-stop to expose the contents of the truck. Their relentless pursuit to salvage the grain was exemplary of the Sudanese of Darfur. After 2 hours, a shovel strikes a metal container and echoes through the wadi.

"Tell the workers to stop digging." I said.

The workers crawl from the hole as Mahdi and myself climb into the opening. We take shovels and very carefully expose a large metal drum. Thoughts of nuclear waste began to race through my mind. Have we finally found the wolf that's been plaguing my thoughts?

Very slowly, we remove all the silt and dirt from around a large drum, exposing her contents. Written in large letters was inscribed "Diesel." Digging beneath this container, we find additional drums of fuel. I am relieved it was only fuel. I breathed a sigh of relief, as we excavate each of the drums. I open each one making sure the contents was diesel.

The days quickly passed as the bridge neared completion. The workers fought the dangerous heat day after day, to finish their lifeline to the world. The completion of the bridge meant we must move further into remote desert region. The souk trucks are en-route as we decide to mount out of Zalingei.

"Mr. Richard. Some of the villagers want to go with you, to help with the road." said Mahdi.

"Tell them I appreciate them for being gracious host, and for their help with the bridge. We cannot take anyone with us because of our limited resources."

"Some of them cried during the night saying they want you to stay."

"Tell them we will pass through here again when our job is complete."

We cross the large Gabian basket bridge, as the villagers stand along side, waving goodbye. I will miss the kindness expressed by these precious souls.

We are ordered to begin building roads to the north into a vast, remote area. A number of small villages affected by the famine occupy this area. Sudan is the ninth largest country in the world, but only ranks 32nd, in population. A large area of open land one-forth the size of the United States.

The sandy soil surrounding us is poorly suited for crop raising. This along with 7 years of drought has led to massive starvation in the region. The most noticeable feature is the absence of perennial streams. The villagers must remain within reach of permanent wells. A number of animal carcasses from cattle, horses, and camel are scattered about as we push into this treacherous terrain.

7
AMBUSH IN THE SAND

We're several miles north of Zalingei, racing toward the village of Tella. We stop to refuel on the edge of a small hillside. I park under a small tree filled with monkeys who appear to be sleeping. Attempting to catch one became futile, as they suddenly awake and begin jumping around.

"Have the workers circle the equipment, and we'll camp here for the night."

"We need to change the blades today. This'll give them the time needed before dark." said Mahdi.

We camp near a small wadi. We dig into the dry creek bed in search for water. A number of date trees nearby yield no fruit. I will survive on a small sack of guava, until we reach the next village.

"When do you expect the next shipment of food to arrive?" asked Mahdi.

"I'll have to guess within the next 3 days."

"This is a harsh region with a hard surface. It's beginning to take a toil on the equipment."

"A fuel truck and a few spare parts will be in this convoy. We'll push into Tella in the next 2 days and wait for the trucks to arrive."

"When do you plan to return to Nyala?" he asked.

"I'm going to stay out here as long as necessary. I don't want any of the shipments to pass without our inspection. Now that the rain has stopped the convoys will increase in number. We want to stay ahead of them, but we'll keep a close watch on everything entering our area."

"The entire crew is happy with the way your handling everything. Not a single one of them wants to quit."

"Tell them we'll begin at daylight in the morning. I want a full 12 hour day tomorrow."

"We'll be ready to move at day break."

I decide to sleep in the rear of the land rover. Gazing at the bright stars overhead, I began to think about home. Without radio, television, newspaper, or any form of communication life takes on a new meaning. The largest concern is finding water each day, along with a small amount of food. I try not to think about the traditional restaurant buffet, with all the trimmings. I drift in and out of sleep as the mosquitoes begin to feed.

We push towards the village, the entire 12 hours, without seeing any sign of life. The terrain is very hilly with limited amounts of water or vegetation. The strewn remains of animals, litter the desert as we approach the village. We must camp another night in the barren terrain. We haven't found any sign of life in the past 2 days.

We start once again, at daybreak, to reach the village. As the noon hour approaches, we see the walls surrounding Tella. The village is small with a large number of refugees nestled inside. Many have fled the hill country in search of food.

The entire village has emerged to greet us. Their small, frail bodies produce a smile, as they barely manage enough strength to stand. The arms and legs of the villagers, says everything. Old, and young alike have suffered tremendously from the ongoing famine.

"Circle the equipment near the hilltop." I said.

"I'll secure everything." said Mahdi.

I walk through the tiny grass huts as the elders resume lying on small mats. The flies, covering them as soon as they become motionless. The stench of death is prevalent, as a number of lifeless bodies lie strewn in the streets. The people, too weak to bury their dead, as they near the same fate.

"Mr. Richard. I have secured the equipment." said Mahdi.

"Take one of the dozers and push a trench on that adjacent hillside. Tell the crew to begin moving the bodies to that site. Do you have any grain left among the crew?"

"Yes. A couple of sacks."

"Have the crew unload the grain and give it to the Shak."

"I'll get the crew moving."

The crew filed past with over a dozen members of the village. We pay our respect as the villagers are laid to rest. Very quietly, the crew covers their remains, as the food is shared among the survivors.

"Do you think the trucks will arrive soon?" asked Mahdi.

"They should be en-route as we speak. The orders I received, said this is the next projected delivery site."

"I hope they arrive soon. There is nothing left for the crew."

A cry for help can be heard in the distance. A lone rider and camel appear, from the barren terrain, in a state of panic. He leaps to the ground and begins to speak rapidly in Arabic.

"What's he saying?" I asked.

"Mr. Richard, He says he saw the convoy approximately 60 kilometers [35-miles] from here. He says the trucks have been shot up by bandits. Many of the drivers shot and the grain is gone. What are we going to do?"

"Ask the Shak if he has any weapons?"

"The Shak says he has none, but the military has a small outpost over the next ridge." said Mahdi.

"Let's go!" I shouted.

Mahdi and I start toward the small outpost. A dozen soldiers man the small army post, armed with AK-47 rifles.

"Tell them we need soldiers to go with us."

"They say they'll send 2 men" he shouted.

The 2 soldiers leap into the land rover with automatic weapons. We drive through the dusty road, not knowing what to expect.

This food shipment is one of the most important to date. I began to think, this was only a dream and I would soon awake, and this would all go away.

As the trucks came into view, it soon became a reality. The trucks were shot up and grain strewn about as the bandits took little time unloading it. We walk through the convoy looking for survivors or anything we could salvage. Suddenly, a shot rang out just overhead. We crawl beneath a souk truck as the shots landed nearby. Apparently, several of the bandits had returned to the area.

The 2 Sudanese soldiers began to engage the bandits with automatic weapons fire. They spray the hills with their AK-47's. After a few moments of silence, the fire resumed from overhead, as they continue to engage us in battle. The two soldiers charged the hillside, firing as they went. The bandits pulled back, breaking off the engagement. Looking into the lower part of the valley, I spot the fuel tanker.

"Look Mahdi, there's the fuel truck, still intact."

"They tried to drive it away but got stuck in the sand." he said.

"We've got to retrieve the fuel truck or we'll be stuck out here for a long time."

"It's sitting on the frame." he said.

"Take the land rover and a soldier and go get the equipment."

"O.K." he said.

He ran to the land rover and stopped suddenly. Turning, he begins to motion for me to come over. Walking toward the land rover, I see the problem. Every tire on it is flat, and we only have one spare.

"Stay here with one of the soldiers. I'll take the other and go for help." I said.

"Mr. Richard, it's over 30 miles to the camp, and the heat's over a hundred degrees. I'll go, so you stay."

"We'll be back before dark. Tell the soldiers what we're going to do. Ask if either one speaks English."

"Neither one can speak English. This soldier says he will go with you." said Mahdi.

"O.K. We'll be back by dark, with help. If the bandits return, don't do anything foolish. That's an order!" I said.

"O.K., we'll wait for you."

We start down the long dusty road towards the village. The Sudanese soldier, takes the assault rifle, and slings it over his shoulder. The sun is blistering hot as we begin the long journey. The heat began taking a toil, after we walk several miles without water. No shade trees to rest under, only hot sand burning our feet as we make our way. We pass several carcasses of animals that had tried to make this journey. The long treacherous walk became unbearable, as we both begin to search for water. Hour after hour, we pressed toward the village. Pointing toward a small ravine, I turned to the soldier, and said,

"Moya." [water]

"Moya moffy." [water none] he said.

The long grueling hours in the desert heat were sheer misery. I decided to get down on both knees in the praying position to rest. He followed suit, as we placed our heads toward the ground. The heat is burning my face, neck and blistered lips. I try to speak, but no words will come from my parched throat.

His face is turning green as he slides face down on the desert floor. Neither of us can utter a single word. I suddenly realize that we could both die, in the middle of nowhere. I lower my head, asking God to please help us. After a few minutes we crawl to our feet stumbling, as we try to walk. The soldier slips, falls and tries to cry out. I pick up the rifle, take him by the arm, and begin to walk once again. We're making one small step at a time. I silently prayed once again, "Lord help us."

We walk several miles, and fall once again, and begin to crawl. I'm becoming delirious as my thoughts ran together. Our bodies have become so dehydrated, that we're no longer perspiring. The color seems to have vanished from our faces. We crawl a few meters and rest, placing our face into the sand, once again. I try to tell myself I'm not thirsty. The blistering sun, and desert sand is very near to claiming two more of it's victims. I began to wonder, how many others have suffered this same fate, in search of food and water in Western Darfur.

We have walked and crawled for more than 8 hours in the 100 plus degrees. We manage to cover only a few meters at a time before resting. It'll take sheer determination to complete the mission. I notice a huge boulder sitting to our right. I remember seeing the large rock before entering the village. I point towards the large boulder and the soldier nods his head. I realize, he knows how close we are to the village. He limps, and falls as his feet have became swollen and bleeding.

We rest once more, as we remain speechless. I began to draw a picture in the sand of the village. I point in the direction straight ahead, and he nods in agreement. We are so close, only if we can just hold out a little longer. We manage to prop against one another as we stagger down the long hill. We're within a couple of miles of the village. Darkness has overtaken us, as we struggle toward the village.

We stagger through the darkness, trying to find our way. We kneel, once again from the excruciating pain, that raced through our bodies. I feel blood seeping from beneath my feet, from blisters coming apart. We try once again to make our way, in the darkness, as we trip and fall. We begin to crawl on our hands and knees. Our condition is critical as we fight for every drop of strength.

Suddenly, we see a camp fire in the village. We continue to crawl on our hands and knees with everything we can muster. A feeling of relief came over us, knowing we're going to survive. The minutes seemed like hours, as we clawed our way through the darkness.

As we make our way into the camp, we're surrounded by soldiers and the entire work crew. A soldier pulls the AK-47 from my shoulder. A feeling of great joy rushed through my body.

Voices in Arabic, can be heard all around, speaking very fast. Suddenly, water is being poured in our mouths as we fight to drink. The workers, gently lift me from the desert floor, and began to carry me. They place me in the tent, with several containers of water. The soldier is placed next to me on a mat. We're to exhausted to move.

I hear the sound of trucks leaving the area at a high rate of speed. Only one worker has stayed, keeping an eye on us. I drift in and out of sleep, wrestling with the agonizing pain, racing through my body.

I know Mahdi, and the remaining soldier, must believe we have fallen prey to the heat. I pray for their safe return. The desert refuses to show mercy to all who cross her path.

The sound of gun fire can be heard in the distance. The convoy of work trucks carrying the soldiers to the ambush site, was suddenly ambushed. The bandits apparently think another shipment of grain is passing through. There's nothing I can do, but lie here and wait. The gun fire lasted for about a half hour, and then, silence.

Several hours passed and I hear the sound of approaching vehicles. The long convoy of souk and work trucks, along with the fuel tanker, arrives in the village. The sound of jubilation can be heard, as the soldiers and work crew dismounted the trucks. A sigh of relief suddenly came over me. I wait in great anticipation to hear Mahdi's voice. The front of the tent flew open as he ran into the tent.

"Mr. Richard, are you alright?"

"Yes, other than a few aches and pains, I'm fine. What happened after we left?"

"Each time we began to try and free the fuel tanker, the bandits would take pot shots at us."

"Were any of the men hurt in the fire fight?"

"Two soldiers, and a driver were slightly wounded."

"These are tough soldiers. This poor guy refused to give up today. Ask him if he's alright?"

"He says he'll be ready for duty tomorrow."

"I wish we could communicate with the bandits in the hills. We'll give them food, if they'll just come into the village."

"They don't want to share with the villagers. They want all of it." said Mahdi.

"I'm not sure if the next shipment is being sent here. Many of the drivers might refuse to enter this area. This entire village will die if we don't do something."

"What do we need to do?" asked Mahdi.

"Did you fix all the flats on the land rover?"

"Yes. It's parked outside."

"We'll take soldiers tomorrow, and head south in search of another convoy." I said.

"I'll find volunteers to go with us."

"Thanks, Mahdi. You did a great job out there today. I appreciate all you're hard work."

"Everyone is willing to stay, because they see your determination to feed the villagers. We'll stay as long as you're out here." he said.

The following morning, I manage to crawl from the cot, and wrap the skin, torn from the blisters. The soreness from the missing skin is almost unbearable. Large water blisters dot my exposed skin and seared lips. My throat is so swollen I can hardly speak. The Sudanese soldier, who walked along side in the desert, began to move around. He's suffering from sheer exhaustion and dehydration. I notice Mahdi heading straight toward the tent.

"Mr. Richard. What do you want to do with this soldier?"

"Ask him if he will allow you to drive him to his base camp?"

"He said he would like that very much." said Mahdi.

"Have several of the workers carry him to the land rover."

"How many soldiers do you want me to ask their commander to assist us?"

"Ask for 2 soldiers to accompany us through the area."

I watch as Mahdi and soldier drive out of site. I am thankful we both survived this traumatic ordeal.

We must have a food delivery in this area, and soon. The small frail bodies of the villagers are almost lifeless. There's little movement coming from the village, as time comes to a standstill in Tella, Sudan.

I forget the pain in my body, and rejoice that I'm alive, after seeing the many tragic sights of those who have perished in the onslaught of famine. Suffering is a way of life for the people of Darfur. There's no easy ride at any level. Every day is a struggle to stay alive, as no health care is available for the many diseases that plague the area. Even dysentery is often as fatal as any major illness.

Mahdi returned with 2 soldiers who have volunteered to travel with us, in search of another convoy. We must act fast before the village of Tella becomes a ghost town.

"Mahdi, have our drivers mount up the souk trucks. We'll return them to Nyala, and bring the food ourselves if necessary. We'll take the lead, with the soldiers."

"I'll get them ready."

We pull the long convoy of souk trucks out onto the road heading south. We ride through the edge of hill country, passing the area the trucks were ambushed earlier in the week. We scan the hills for bandits, but all is quiet. The long, dusty road shows no sign of life in the barren terrain.

Only an occasional vulture can be seen circling overhead. We stop at a small water hole dug in the wadi. Several of the trucks are overheating as the desert takes its toil. We continue for several hours, passing the village of Zalingei once again. The Gabian bridge remains intact as the villagers lining her, wave as we pass. We continue to search in vain, for another convoy en-route.

The sun is beginning to set, as darkness falls in Western Darfur. We've been on the road for over 12 hours. We stop at a small wadi and camp for the night. We'll try to reach Nyala by noon tomorrow.

There's only silence in the camp, as the workers refuse to complain about their lack of food.

At daylight we are on the road, once again. After 6 hours of hard driving, we enter the town of Nyala. We stop at the railroad, seeing no sign of life. We enter the small depot, finding a man asleep on the floor.

"Mahdi, find out what has happened to the food shipments."

"He says the railroad was washed out from the floods and never rebuilt." said Mahdi.

"Ask him how the grain is being shipped?"

"He says it's all coming by truck from Khartoum."

"Ask him, when the next shipment is due?"

"He said maybe tomorrow."

"Tell the drivers to dismount and prepare to stay here tonight."

"I'll tell them." he said.

"Let's go to Arkel-Talab's office."

8
NOT BY BREAD ALONE

Arriving, we find a British Diplomat visiting from the United Kingdom. He is introduced and goes into great detail about the famine relief operation. He's especially concerned about the lack of coordination at every level.

"What is your job?" he asked.

"I'm Field Supervisor for road building in Darfur." I answered.

"How is the road building going?"

"The road building is ahead of the food shipments." I answered.

"How far would you say the road extends?"

"We have built over 600 kilometers [360 miles] of pioneer dirt roads."

"What type of construction is involved in completion of these roads?"

"We are currently using 2 African construction companies. We are operating with approximately 60% of necessary manpower and equipment. I believe we can manage to stay ahead of the shipments now that the railroad is in-operative."

"How many of the villages have been supplied with food, since your operation began?"

"Over a dozen villages, with thousands of refugees from neighboring Chad. The additional refugees place a tremendous burden on the local villagers."

"When do you plan to resume your road construction?"

"We will leave as soon as the next shipment arrives in Nyala. This shipment has to reach a village north of Zalingei, and soon."

"May I accompany you on this journey?" he asked.

"I would be more than happy to have you along."

I leave the room in search of Mahdi. I find him with the mechanic, who has placed a new set of tires on the land rover. I call him outside the compound to tell him the news.

"We're going to have an added guest tomorrow. A British Diplomat is going to drill us for information. We know nothing about the nuclear waste if asked. We'll only talk about the road building."

"I understand Mr. Richard." he said.

"I want you to take the land rover and return to the railroad. Report back as soon as they arrive."

"Yes sir."

The baboon, at the front door has been relocated to the rear of the building. It was done at the request of our new guest. I notice he has became quite aggressive since I last saw him.

"Richard, I need to talk with you." said Ronnie.

"Sure." I answered.

"How's everything going in the bush?"

"As well as can be expected."

"Did the newspaper reporter ever catch up with you?"

"Yes. He was relentless in his pursuit."

"What did he tell you?"

"Probably the same thing he told you." I answered.

"What's your opinion on the subject?"

"I'm here to build the road and help with the food deliveries, nothing more."

"Look, just don't get in the way. Just continue on like your going, O.K." he said.

"You have nothing to worry about."

"Thanks. I know I can depend on you." he said.

"When is the next food shipment arriving?" I asked.

"First thing in the morning." he said.

"Excellent. We'll escort it into the northern area."

"We're invited to a meeting tonight, to join with other members of various relief agencies from the EEC."

"Do you plan on going?" I asked.

"No way. They'll tear you to ribbons when they find out your a yank." he said.

"I think we should know what the other people are doing." I said.

"You're going to show up?"

"Yes. I'm a little curious about what they're going to say." I answered.

At 6 P.M. I arrive at the same small office where I had picked up the map, months earlier. Some of the same faces were present I had seen on my last visit. Conversations were abundant as everyone swapped stories about the famine. The only problem is everyone is completely ignoring me. I've been invited so I'm not leaving until it's time. Some of the stories were of the horrific sights encountered in Darfur. Suddenly, without warning, an Australian turns to me an said, "What are you guys doing to help out?"

"We're doing everything possible to get the food to the out lying villages." I answered.

"Sure you are. Did you hear that folks? Arkel-Talab is now making food deliveries."

The laughter almost brought the house down. Each one in unison threw dart piercing insults at me. I knew I would encounter resentment but not on this scale. I was glad Ronnie wasn't present tonight.

"We know what your doing in Darfur, and we don't like it, so get out." he said.

Without saying another word I left, and walk back to the office. Ronnie watched me enter and followed me into the rear of the building.

"You weren't gone very long." he said.

"Yes, it was time to go." I said.

"I know they're like a bunch of rabid dogs. They attack me everyday, without any provocation."

"I was hired to do a job. I refuse to get involved in their rivalry."

"I know they spend most of their time in Nyala, and not in the bush." said Ronnie.

"My only concern is whether the food convoy arrives tomorrow. We're not stopping until it reaches Tella."

"The British Diplomat wants to go with you. Make sure he doesn't make you say something you'll regret later." he said.

"I'll be on my best behavior, O.K. What about a radio so we can keep in contact?"

"Sorry, the company doesn't have and extra one." he said.

"I'll manage to get by without one."

The following morning, Mahdi pulls into the compound. The souk trucks have arrived with a dozen trucks loaded with grain. I tell the British Diplomat we are ready to depart Nyala.

"I'm sorry, I should have told you last evening. Princess Anne will be arriving today from the U.K. I must remain and greet her." he said.

"Please tell the Princess I'm a fan of hers. I only wish I could have escorted her into the surrounding area." I said.

"Cheers mate, and have a safe trip." he said.

"Let's go Mahdi."

We pull into the railroad station to inspect the trucks. They're loaded with sorghum, stacked over the cab. We climb aboard each truck to check the grain.

"It looks like a food shipment, so let's roll." I said.

We lead the convoy, as we follow the winding road out of Nyala. We leave the empty souk trucks, brought from Tella, placing our drivers in the loaded souk trucks with the new drivers. The 2 soldiers are riding in the land rover with us. It will take approximately 18 hours, nonstop to make the trip. We will not stop even if the bandits try to rob the trucks. The drivers have been warned not to stop for any reason.

"What kind of food did Ronnie give you, to survive on?" asked Mahdi.

"Water chestnuts." I answered.

"What kind of food is that?" he asked.

"I've never seen any before. I didn't know what to do with them."

"Where are they now?" he asked.

"I poured them into the baboons food bowl."

"What did he do with them."

"He began throwing them, so I knew I didn't want them."

"What did the Diplomat want?" he asked.

"Do either of these soldiers speak English?" I asked.

"No. I tried to speak to them both in English and they didn't have a clue."

"The Diplomat wanted to go into the bush with us. I believe he's heard the horror stories, and he's trying to bust this operation wide open."

"What are we going to do when we arrive in Tella."

"We'll continue to head north until we receive a change of orders. We'll search every shipment that enters our area." I said.

"What about a radio?" he asked.

"We'll never receive a radio. I've only gotten a lot of excuses. I believe we are purposely being kept in the dark."

We travel the long dusty road until late in the afternoon. We stop and refuel all vehicles, so we have no excuse to stop after dark. The bandits operate freely near the hill country, so we'll take no chances.

All containers are filled to capacity with water. We are underway in less than a half-hour.

We are within a couple of hours of the village of Tella. It will be dark as we pass through the previous ambush site.

The trucks are bunched up as darkness covers Darfur.

"We are within a few miles of the ambush site. Tell the soldiers to be alert."

"They say they're ready."

"I want you to speed up and the trucks will follow suit."

"O.K." he said.

We have the land rover at top speed. The souk trucks are following close behind, in the giant dust cloud.

We pass the previous ambush site with no trouble. We finally arrive at Tella, around mid-night. The villagers rise to the occasion, as they meet the trucks. Their frail bodies surround the vehicles with open arms. I breathed a sigh of relief as I enter the tent, exhausted. I will rest, knowing the survivors of Tella, Sudan will live another day.

Daylight came very early as the crew began to stir. The cool morning breeze makes one forget he's in the desert. The entire crew is facing towards Mecca, face down, on their prayer mats. Today is Friday, so no work will be performed by the Muslims. I decide to build a small shower in the rear of the tent. It has been almost a month since my last bath. I wait until after dark to erect the shower. Taking the flashlight, I commence to construct a small platform.

"What are you doing?" asked Mahdi.

"I borrowed a 5 gallon water bag in Nyala, so I'm building a temporary shower."

"What do I need to do?" he asked.

"Climb up on that tree limb and hang the bag upside down."

"Do you have enough water to fill it?" he asked.

"Yes, in this metal drum." I answered.

"You dip and I'll pour from up here." he said.

"There's barely enough water to fill it so I'll tip the drum over."

I hand Mahdi the flashlight, and began to tip the drum over. Wearing sandals, I place my right foot under the drum. Suddenly, there's a movement under my foot, as something begins to slap against my leg. I drop the drum, and run backward several feet.

"What's the matter, Mr. Richard?"

"There's something under the drum. Bring the flashlight and we'll have a look."

"You shine the light and I'll see what's under it." said Mahdi.

He grabbed a shovel and stood at my side. I quickly flip the drum over, and Mahdi screams out.

"Black Cobra!"

My heart began pounding as the 6-foot deadly serpent began striking with a vengeance. The sandal marks of dust dotted his head, making him very angry. Taking the shovel, Mahdi cut him into several pieces. He then placed him in the large campfire nearby.

"Are you alright, Mr. Richard!"

"Ask me in a couple of minutes. That was too close for me." I answered.

"Did he bite you?"

"No, by the Grace of God, I've been spared."

"Your sandal had been placed on his head miraculously. If not, you would be dead now." he said.

"I better sit down."

"You must serve the True God." he said.

"Thank you Jesus." I answered.

"Thank you Jesus." he replied.

I was truly thankful to have survived the ordeal. Cobras inhabit an extreme geographic range within Africa. They'll bite unpredictably with grave tissue destruction with neurological effect. The Black Cobra has the ability of atomizing venom accurately to a distance of 20 feet. Their bite is often fatal, as a result of the lack of medical facilities available.

The area surrounding Tella, has suffered greatly from the flooding. The terrain is practically impassable as we try to push into the north country. We spend the morning hours placing laterite, an excellent filler, into the local area to help future shipments traveling through. We scout ahead of the equipment, marking the trail to follow. We stop at a small wadi in search of water. Only a small number of dead trees, and strewn carcasses are visible. No shaded areas can be found, to escape the blistery heat. I walk around a small hillside, spotting a large tree laying upon its side. It looks to be over a hundred years old by the many rings inside. A large number of holes were visible as I observed its massive size.

"I wouldn't get too close if I were you." said Mahdi.

"Why not?" I asked.

"That's a snake den." he answered.

"How can you be sure?"

"You see the trails in the sand around it. Those are probably large cobras living inside." he said.

"What other type of deadly snakes inhabit this area?" I asked.

"We have several types of snakes. One is the Sand Boa, who hides himself just beneath the sand. We've also got the dreaded Gaboon Viper, that displays a scaly horn on its head. They have very long fangs, about 2 inches in length. The Gaboon Viper will not release it's prey until it's victim dies. If it's threatened, it will raise the upper part of his body and hiss before striking. If he's hungry, he'll strike at any movement near him. We've also got the Rhino-horned viper, Desert horned viper and several species of deadly scorpions." he said.

"What does the Gaboon viper resemble?" I asked.

"He looks a lot like your American rattlesnake. They grow to about 7 feet in length, and are thick bodied. He has a very wide head, and is marked in diamonds and stripes."

"Do you know of anyone who's been bitten by one of these snakes?" I asked.

"Yes, several family members have died as a result of these deadly snakes. My oldest brother was bitten by a cobra as he gathered firewood. He managed to tell my sister what happened before he went into a comma and died." he said.

"I'm sorry I asked, Mahdi?"

"No, don't be sorry, we all suffer defeat sometimes." he said.

"Do you come from a large family?" I asked.

"Yes, I have 11 brothers and sisters, and my mother and father are dead."

"Where were you born?"

"El Obeid." he answered.

"How did you come about with your present job with Africa Construction?"

"I learned English from a British missionary who came to El Obeid when I was a child. Many of the locals refused to attend school because of their hatred of the British." he said.

"Why did they hate the British?" I asked.

"We won our independence from them and wanted to return to the days of Sultans in Sudan. We wanted our old style of religion back. Outsiders were shunned because of what the Muslim religion taught about white people."

"What did your Muslim religion teach you about white people?" I asked.

"We were taught that the devil is white, and all of his children are white. We were taught that God is black and all his true children are black." he said.

"What do you believe?" I asked.

"I believe that God is neither black nor white. I only know that white people have always came to help us when we needed assistance. The missionary was the kindest person I've ever known. I loved her as a mother."

"What happened to her?"

"She died with malaria after suffering many days with high fever. I had to leave the school and find work. I became an equipment operator in Southern Sudan. Speaking English landed me a job as a foreman, and I ended up out here." he said.

"I'm glad you're here Mahdi. The workers respond to your orders, which makes my job much easier."

"They respond because they respect what you're doing for our people." he said.

"Let's go find the equipment." I said.

The dust can be seen for miles as the dozers push through the rugged terrain. The workers refuse to stop as their faces are covered with dust and sweat. They continue to build the pioneer road until we reach the small wadi we had found

139

earlier in the day.

The following morning, after the prayer mats are rolled up, the workers began to refuel their equipment.

The long line of tipper trucks began to roll across the wadi, followed by scrapers and graders, to begin moving a large laterite deposit on the adjacent hill.

"Mahdi, have the dozer operators meet us over at that large snake den."

"Yes sir." he said.

I walk over to the ancient tree lying next to the wadi. A long black tail is protruding from one of the holes in its side. I stand back approximately 50 feet from the den. The sound of the tracks on the large dozers echoes in the hilly terrain. The rumble increases as they near the site.

"Tell one of the dozer operators to dig out a large hole in the wadi. Have the other operator bring his dozer around to this side." I said.

"O.K." said Mahdi.

The large blade began to carve a deep ravine in the wadi near the tree. The long black tail, quickly disappeared inside the recesses of the ancient tree. Within a few minutes, I give the order to stop digging. I have both dozers line up alongside the other.

"Push the snake den into the ravine and bury it." I said.

The order was given and the two giant D-8 dozers dropped the blades at the base of the tree. The tracks rumbled as they began pushing the giant tree into the deep ravine. It hit with a loud boom, as it rolled to the bottom, and dozens of large snakes began to crawl out. The large blades continued to push and roll over the ravine until nothing escaped.

"Tell them to rejoin the rest of the crew, and let's get underway."

"O.K." said Mahdi.

We will continue northwest to the small village of Dei. The terrain is extremely dry and stony, with rolling hills. We haven't seen another human being since leaving Tella. A few carcasses from small animals dot the countryside. Around mid-afternoon we find another small wadi, as we scout ahead. Digging several feet in the center, we find water. A precious resource, limited in quantity, that is greatly desired above riches in Western Darfur.

The equipment arrives and is placed in a close circle. The workers build a large campfire as they prepare another meal of sorghum. The morale remains very high as we enter the most remote region we've encountered thus far.

"How do you like this American sorghum?" asked Mahdi.

"I'd prefer it better with a little cheese." I laughed.

"What do you use sorghum for in America?" he asked.

"We feed this to our cattle."

"Wow, those are some special cows to eat this good." he said.

"How much grain do you have left for the crew?"

"Another few days at the most." he said.

"I'm expecting another shipment in a couple of days. We should be near the village of Dei tomorrow night. We'll stay put until it arrives."

"Where do you think we'll be going next?"

"The orders I have, say to remain at Dei for additional orders. I'm sure we'll know in a couple days."

"I have reminded the crew we'll begin Ramadan in 2

days." he said.

"We'll be in the village so it won't be as hard on them. I want them to carry additional water for the day time." I said.

"We'll fill every spare container to capacity."

"O.K., we'll start again at daybreak."

The word Ramadan means "scorcher" in Arabic. The Muslim people will eat no food during daylight hours for 40 days. They will drink only water in the day time, while eating only at night. The followers of Ramadan claim this time "may cultivate piety". The day doesn't occur on the same day each year. The new moon signals the beginning of Ramadan. It must be reported by 2 trustworthy witnesses. Ramadan can begin and end on different dates in different parts of the world. As a result of a 354 day calendar year in the Islamic world, this event takes place 11 days earlier each year.

"Mahdi, do you observe Ramadan?" I asked.

"No." he said.

"I suggest we don't eat in front of the crew during daylight hours, to help maintain morale."

9
COVER OF DARKNESS

The dozers take the lead once again as we're en-route to the village of Dei. We find plenty of materials to smooth the road for the souk trucks to follow. Around 10 A.M. the temperatures soar above the 100 degree mark. We take the land rover and scout ahead, finding no life as we roam the countryside. After several hours of searching the hilly terrain we stop to wait on the equipment.

Walking around the scorched, dusty terrain, I find a few animal bones scattered about. We dig for water, in several spots in the wadi, before finding a small amount. We quickly begin filling everything that held water, just in case we run into any trouble up ahead. The water begins to slow as we're forced to did deeper to find it.

The equipment has arrived, so we scout ahead marking the road, while searching for the village. Across the bumpy terrain, void of life, we continue to search. We find a winding camel trail coming from the adjacent hills. We decide to follow it, believing it will lead us to the village. After a couple of arduous hours of sheer punishment, we see the grass huts coming into view.

"Do you want to drive into the village?" asked Mahdi.

"No. We'll enter her tonight with the entire crew. We don't want to walk into a possible ambush by bandits." I answered.

"I forgot about them." he said.

"Let's go find the equipment."

The equipment is only a couple of hours away from the village. If everything goes as planned, we should reach her before dark. The excellent materials in the area allow the crew to build the road at a faster pace.

Without stopping the crew arrives in the village an hour before sundown.

The famine ravaged people stand next to a small grass wall as we enter. We find the familiar scene of skin and bones, with a stench of death in the air. Circling the equipment, we enter the small village that has survived more than her share of hardships. The horrible scenes cannot be described in words. I'm not sure a food shipment now will be able to save anyone. I only wished we had arrived at least a week earlier.

"Take a dozer and dig a hole on that ridge." I said.

"Yes sir." said Mahdi.

The workers began burying the dead, beginning with the village Shak. We pay our last respect as the graves are covered. The crew encircled the area with stones as we await the arrival of the convoy. The silence of the village is almost unbearable. Not a single sound emitted from within the grass covered walls. The villagers hold onto life as they await their fate.

The silence is broken in the early morning hours, as the sound of trucks can be heard in the distance. I walk outside the tent to witness the approaching headlights. The crew began to stir as the trucks arrived, and prepare to unload her cargo. I hear a voice calling me from the darkness.

"Mr. Richard, I'm ready to search the trucks." cried Mahdi.

"We'll start with the lead truck." I said.

We climb aboard and begin to unload the cargo, as we discreetly began our search. The workers were carrying the sorghum inside the village walls, for the malnourished survivors of Dei. We climb from truck to truck, relentless in our pursuit. Finally, we climb aboard the last truck, pushing several sacks from the center, over to one side. Suddenly a voice speaks from the shadows in English saying,

"Hope you find everything in order."

I froze, and turned around quickly, shining the light to the rear of the convoy. A late model land cruiser was parked a few meters to the rear of the convoy, observing our operation. Two white men emerged and began walking slowly toward us.

"Who are they Mr. Richard?" whispered Mahdi.

"Spooks, nothing more." I replied.

"Who's in command here?" they asked.

"I am." I replied.

"I've got orders for you, from Khartoum. May we join you in you quarters?"

"Sure, follow me."

I notice both men are wearing identical clothing. Both are wearing desert tan hats, kaki pants, shirts, and desert tan boots. The elder, in his early fifties, is sporting a beard. The younger, in his early thirties, and clean shaven. Entering the tent I'm handed a large amount of paperwork from Khartoum.

"What brings you 2 guys into this remote region?"

"We're doctors." they replied.

"Doctors, that's great. I've been sick lately. Maybe you guys can give me a check-up."

"Maybe so, but we've got an awful lot of work to do first." they replied.

"What kind of work are you going to be doing?" I asked.

"We'll be checking all the surrounding villages for Aids patients."

"Have you found a lot of Aids patients in Sudan?"

"Sure, over 50 percent of our patients have tested positive for Aids." they replied.

"That's incredible to find such a large number in such a remote area." I said.

"Where are you guys from?" I asked.

"Brooklyn."

"Both of you from Brooklyn, what a coincidence."

"We'll be here for a few days." they said.

"You're the only 2 American doctors I've seen in Sudan. The EEC has Doctors without Borders, but no Americans." I said.

"Yes, I'm sure they'll be more Americans out here before we're through." they said.

"That would be great, more Americans."

146

"May we stay in your quarters tonight?" they asked.

"Sure, you fellows make yourself at home. I'll stay with the crew tonight." I replied.

I left them in the tent, joining Mahdi in the camp. The crew has finished unloading the sorghum, and the souk trucks are returning to Nyala.

"Who are they Mr. Richard?" asked Mahdi.

"Mahdi these guys claim to be doctors, but have no medical equipment. They're spooks and very poor liars. I've got a stack of new orders from Khartoum. We'll go over them at daylight. We've got to keep a close watch on these guys."

"What are spooks Mr. Richard?"

"C. I. A." I answered.

"What are we going to do?" he asked.

"I'll guarantee the new orders are for us to leave immediately. They'll be too anxious to see us go. We're going to stall for time by dragging our feet. I want every piece of equipment stalled for the next few days."

"I'll take care of that for you." he said.

"Thanks Mahdi."

The following morning all equipment is down for servicing. There's no sound coming from the tent. I decide to look around their land cruiser. Inside are several pieces of communication equipment, one with a small satellite dish. Returning to the campfire, I proceed to open our new orders.

It reads, "Richard, you will leave the 2 D-8 dozers and operators in Dei. You will proceed north to El Fasher with the other crew members and equipment. You will commence building a new road to El Geneina. We will send other dozers as they become available."

This makes absolutely no sense, I thought. The relief operation is going very well, and isn't close to being complete. It will take at least 3 additional months to cover this area properly. Leaving now meant that thousands of refugees fleeing the famine will starve. I have a sick feeling knowing we'll have to abandon this effort. I take the orders and place them in the fire.

One of our guest began to emerge from the tent. He walks to the land cruiser, and takes one of the radios from the rear of the vehicle. He returns to the tent and proceeds to make radio contact with one of his associates. I walk to the rear of the tent to eavesdrop on the conversation. I have no clue what they're saying, because the wording appears to be in code. I have a plan and they're not going to like it. Suddenly, the 2 men emerge from the tent.

"Have you reviewed your new orders?" they asked.

"Yes sir, where would you like the dozers placed?" I asked.

"Please follow us and we'll show you the area." they said.

"Sure, I'll get my foreman."

I wave for Mahdi to join me, and he ran to meet me at the land rover.

"Where are we going?" he asked.

"Follow that land cruiser." I said.

We drive approximately 5 miles into a large, flat, open area north of the village. They exit the land cruiser and walk a few paces before stopping. We pull along side, and walk toward them.

"Have your operators bring the 2 dozers and park them here."

"Yes sir. I'll have them here in about an hour."

"Excellent." they said.

We return to the vehicle and follow them back to camp. They return to the tent and make radio contact once again, with their associates.

"Tell the dozer operators to follow you to the location and leave the equipment. Return with both operators, A.S.A.P.

"Yes sir." said Mahdi.

Suddenly, the 2 men exit the tent, and walk toward me. They wave for me to join them, as they continued heading in my direction.

"Look, when do you plan on leaving?" they asked.

"I'll have to scout the road tomorrow with my foreman. We'll be ready to move within 2 days."

"Excellent." they said.

"Hey Doc, maybe you could give me a checkup before I leave." I said.

"Uh, uh, sure we'll work you in."

"Thanks Doc. Just let me know, O.K. "I said.

I see Mahdi and the 2 operators, returning to camp. He exits the vehicle and walks toward me.

"Fill the land rover with fuel, and place two drums of fuel in the rear." I said.

"O.K."

After a few minutes Mahdi signals he has everything ready. I place 2 cans of water, and a sleeping bag into the land rover.

"Tell the crew to stay put until we return. I want the mechanic to grab his gear and go with us."

"I'll pass the word." he said.

Within minutes we're out of site, as we turn toward El Fasher. We cross the dry wadi and pass the 2 dozers and enter the remote, barren area once again.

"Where are we going Mr. Richard?" asked Mahdi.

"El Fasher."

"What will we do when we arrive?" he asked.

"We're going to the Sudanese military."

"There's a large tank unit in El Fasher." he said.

"Do they have a general?" I asked.

"Yes sir. He's a very powerful man."

"Great. Take me to him."

We travel the entire morning through rough terrain, before crossing the hill country. We stop only once, to fix a flat, before continuing on our journey.

Around 3 P.M. we enter the town of El Fasher. We weave around several herds of goats and donkeys, as we enter the military base.

Stepping from the land rover, we watch the Sudanese army pass in review. Many of the men are wearing sandals while others are in combat boots. Their uniforms appear to be different shades of green. Only half of them are wearing hats, in a variety of different styles. Each is armed with AK-47 assault rifles.

I look to the rear of the base at a number of tanks, mostly old Russian T-54 and T-55 medium tanks. There's only a couple of old towed artillery pieces, and about a dozen military trucks and jeeps.

A Sudanese army officer approached us and began speaking to Mahdi. After a short conversation he points to a small building.

"Mr. Richard, he says the general is behind those doors, and he'll take us to him."

"Let's go." I said.

We walk to a small green building, stopping at the door. The officer knocks, and a voice from inside calls out. The officer slowly opens the door and we walk inside. Behind a small desk sits the general. A rather large man, with a receding hairline, and plenty of military decorations dotting his uniform. He smiles and invites us to sit down. Within minutes a woman appears with hot tea. We drink several glasses of hot tea with the general, before he asked what we're doing in El Fasher.

"He wants to know what he can do for us." said Mahdi.

"Tell the general I have 2 drums of fuel for his jeep." I said.

"The general says he likes a white man with gifts like this. Now he says he wants to do something for you."

"Tell the general I would like to bring my equipment to his base. We'll take the G-14 graders and repair the base after the terrible flooding."

"He says you're now a friend of his. He wants to know what he can do for you."

"Tell the general I need 2 tank carriers to bring my equipment to El Fasher."

"He says you can have as many as you need."

"Tell the general I need them today."

"He says we'll drink tea today. You can have them tomorrow morning."

"I'm starting to enjoy this Sudanese tea." I said.

The general turned out to be an excellent host. We were given a private room with a nice army cot to sleep upon. The following morning, we join the general for breakfast. We enjoy eggs, bread, and hot tea, served by his maid.

"The general says the trucks are ready." said Mahdi.

Standing, I salute the general and he stands and returns the salute. A large smile came over his face as we shake hands.

"Tell the general we'll return within 24 hours."

"The general says he has attached 6 infantrymen to protect his new friend."

"Tell him I'm honored to be his friend."

The trucks follow close behind with armed soldiers as we exit the city. We travel nonstop through the dusty terrain. The giant tank carriers are capable of carrying 60 ton tanks. They will have no trouble in moving the equipment.

"If we turn south now, we'll encounter better terrain." said Mahdi.

"Let's go south."

The 100 miles of rough terrain will take approximately 4 hours travel time. We're 2 hours into the trip and a beautiful view comes into sight. A mountain to our right, at least 9,000 feet in height, is covered with green vegetation.

"What is that?" I asked.

"Jabal Marra, the highest mountain in Darfur." answered Mahdi.

"It looks like a volcano."

"It's a dead volcano, with a large crater, filled with animals, trees, and fruit growing year round. Water flows continually from its many fountains." said Mahdi.

"Does anyone live there?"

"Yes, at the very top, lives a Sudanese inventor of various medicines. He has a large family and they never leave the mountain."

"Are there any roads leading to the top?"

"No. Only a small trail, winding around, stretching for many miles. The trip to the top and back, takes 2 days time."

"I'd like to take a trip to the top, but I promised the general we'd return in 24 hours."

"Maybe next time, Mr. Richard."

"Maybe."

The beauty of the mountain fades in the distance. We have entered the rough terrain, once again, for the remainder of the trip. Around noon, we pull alongside the two large D-8 dozers parked 5 miles north of Dei. Stopping the large tank carriers, the troops suddenly dismount.

"Load a dozer on each truck." I said.

"Yes sir." said Mahdi.

The soldiers dropped the loading ramps in the rear of the tank carriers. The mechanic started the engines on both dozers. Mahdi proceeded to drive the giant dozer onto the first tank carrier. The soldiers commence to chain the large tracks, securing it in place. The process was repeated, as the second dozer was loaded and secured.

"Tell the soldiers to take the dozers to the army base. Have the mechanic to accompany them."

"They say they'll have them waiting when you return to the base."

"Great. Let's go see what the doctors are doing."

We pull into the camp at Dei and find the land cruiser and our 2 guests missing.

"Ask the crew where the 2 men have gone."

"They say, both of them headed south 2 hours ago." said Mahdi.

"Excellent. Their probably going to meet some of their friends. Have the crew load the tent."

"Mr. Richard, everything is loaded and ready to go."

"Let's roll, we've got a dinner date tonight with the general."

We take the lead as the long convoy of equipment pulls from the small village of Dei. The poor villagers stand along the small wadi, waving goodbye.

"Mr. Richard, what do you think will happen when they find out we stole the dozers?" asked Mahdi.

"Mahdi, you can't steal something that's already yours." I answered.

"I agree." he said.

"After all, what does a doctor need with a D-8 dozer?"

"Good point, Mr. Richard."

"Let's take the high road around Jabal Marra. I want one final look at her."

"Yes sir." he said.

After crossing the rough terrain, we enter the flat area surrounding Jabal Marra. The splendor of her defies logic. Surrounded by barren, desolate, and useless ground, it sits as an oasis in the desert.

"You've climbed to the top, Mahdi."

"Yes, when I first came to Darfur. You have to carry water, because it has many dry areas. If not, you may not come out alive. There are a number of very steep cliffs you must walk around. You must stay on the path or you'll be lost quickly."

"What did you find at the top?"

"A village with a large family. They grow an abundance of fruit, like oranges, mango, and guava. The people receive nothing from the outside world."

"Have you considered moving there?"

"Yes, but the locals don't allow any outsiders to join them, only visit."

The mountain begins to disappear, once again, as we continue north towards El Fasher. It's mid-afternoon, as we arrive at the army base. Over to the right side of the camp sit the 2 tank carriers and dozers. We're greeted by a Sudanese officer who takes us, once again, to the general. We are quickly served hot tea, as we sit and discuss the things that need to be done.

"The general says he's glad to see us." said Mahdi.

"Tell the general we're ready to repair the base."

"He says we must drink tea before any repairs can be made."

We began to exchange small talk, back and forth, about our operation. We drink tea, for about an hour and finally, the general decided it was time to make repairs.

"He says he's ready."

"Have the 966-loader start at the base of the hill, loading trucks. As soon as the laterite hits the ground, have all G-14 graders leveling their parade deck."

The operation went like clockwork, as the general and I, stood nearby and watched. Within 2 hours the base looked completely new. The foul smell, and washed out furrows were now ready for inspection. I tell Mahdi to secure the equipment as the sun begins to set in Western Darfur.

"The general insist we have dinner with him tonight." said Mahdi.

"Tell him we'd be honored."

Each of the crew members will stay in the barracks with the soldiers. Mahdi and I, are given a private room. Water is brought so we can wash before the evening meal. Within a half hour, we're escorted to the dining room.

"The general says he appreciates the work you've done at the base."

"Tell him, I appreciate the loan of the 2 tank carriers."

"He wants to know where you're going next?"

"Tell him, El Geniena."

"He says it's very dangerous along the 200 mile stretch."

"Tell him we'll be fine."

"He says, he's assigned the 2 tank carriers and 6 soldiers to go with us on our journey."

"Tell him thank you, but I must decline the offer."

"He says, he'll not take no as an answer."

"Tell him they must be ready to leave at daybreak."

"He says they'll be ready."

10
THE BORDER COUNTRY

The following morning, the silence is broken by the roar of engines. The Sudanese soldiers are inside the tank carriers, ready to begin the trip. All the workers are loading onto their equipment as we prepare to leave.

"Mr. Richard, the general says his prayers are with you."

"I'll thank him later, let's take the lead."

We drive pass the guards, as the long convoy begins to rumble into the street. We'll travel approximately 30 miles to the village of Tawilla, and begin the road building. The tank carriers are a real asset to the operation. We will have the ability to move the dozers around at a faster pace.

We arrive at the village around 10 A.M. and unload the dozers. The village has suffered tremendously, according to the size of the graveyard. A large freshly covered mound of dirt spanned the entire rear of the village. The people are mere skeletons, that can no longer feed themselves.

"What do you want to do first?" asked Mahdi.

"Check inside with the Shak. Tell him we're going to dig another large hole behind the village."

"What are we going to dig a large hole for, Mr. Richard?" asked Mahdi.

"Another graveyard." I answered.

A very old man, barely standing, emerges from his hut. He began to speak to Mahdi in a soft voice, shaking his head, as he walked.

"He's the village Shak, and wants the hole dug." said Mahdi.

"Place a dozer behind the graves, and have the other equipment head due west." I said.

"I'll have them begin now." said Mahdi.

The stench from the village was unbearable, as I began to walk some distance away. The Shak continued to speak to Mahdi, for several minutes. I motion to the dozer to stop, pointing for him to join the rest of the crew. We have dug a large gaping hole, big enough for the entire village, if needed.

"Mr. Richard, the Shak said some of those inside the village had fled the famine in El Geneina. They have warned him, that the further west you go, the worst the famine. He said thousands have died between here and the Chadian border. He said some of those in his village were dying from diseases.

"Tell the Shak that food is en-route, so try and hold on as long as possible."

"He says there is little food to eat, and nothing for medicine."

"Tell him the first food shipment should stop in his village, after leaving El Fasher."

"He said this will give his villagers hope."

"We've got to catch up with the crew" I said.

We exit the small village that appears to be extinct. It's getting very difficult looking into the faces, and seeing the pain, that won't go away. This is the most difficult part of the job. I've never imagined a place like this existed on earth. Nothing could have prepared me for this. It seems more like a bad dream, than reality. We're only eating one meal a day, of bread and sorghum. I begin to fill guilty of eating before the starving masses. I will only eat in the dark from henceforth.

The terrain is often impassable for everything, but pack animals. We strive to push inland, but we're rejected by the harsh conditions. We're only moving at a snails pace, because of the deep ravines, and long haul for materials. We're having excessive amounts of down time, due to the extreme terrain.

Over a month has passed since we left, El Fasher. We have seen no food shipments since leaving Dei, 5 weeks earlier. Ramadan has passed, and the crew is working at full speed. The equipment needs to be serviced, as the rugged terrain takes its toil.

We camp near a wadi, in search for water. The crew digs for almost an hour, before finding this much needed resource. Repairs have begun on the equipment, after the severe beating, suffered by the dozers.

Several people from the surrounding area, have entered our camp, foraging for food. We can offer them only a handful of grain, as we run dangerously low ourselves.

We'll attempt to reach the village of Omri, within the next few days. The morale of the crew remains high, as they continue to work without complaint.

We reach a large ravine covered with the carcasses, of man and beast. The vultures are the only survivors, of this horrific scene. It looks like a war zone, with famine as the only weapon, where no winners abound. The entire road crew stops to take in this horrible sight.

"Mahdi, take the equipment, and bury their remains."

"Thanks Mr. Richard, the crew wanted to cover them as well."

"It looks like a large caravan of people had arrived, and just given up."

"It appears they were Chadian, from their clothing." said Mahdi.

"Place large stones around the perimeter, letting others know this is a graveyard."

"I'll tell the crew." said Mahdi.

The vultures continue to defy the workers, as they circle the area. The stench of death covers a large sector, in every direction. As the last stone is placed, around this hallowed ground, we continue to press toward Omri.

We try to scout ahead, but we're forced to turn back each time, because of the rugged terrain. I place a D-8 dozer in the front, to remove every obstacle, between us and the village. After several days of relentless pursuit, the village finally comes into view.

"We'll go just beyond the village, and camp on that adjacent hillside."

"O.K." said Mahdi.

We circle the equipment only a few meters from several small huts. The people ran and hid themselves, as we prepare to camp. The following morning, every hut and occupant has disappeared. Not a single trace of them can be found. They apparently wanted some privacy, and decided to go elsewhere during the night.

"Mahdi, let's enter the village and talk to the Shak."

"O.K. I hope he's friendlier than the ones that left during the night." he said.

We enter the well hidden village nestled next to the wadi. The silence is broken, as Mahdi calls for the Shak. Several minutes pass, as he calls out once again, for anyone. A voice from behind the grass wall begins to speak. After several minutes, Mahdi turned to me saying, "He says they're very sick, and for us to go away."

"What kind of sickness do they have?" I asked.

"He says, high fever."

"Tell them food should be arriving soon."

"He says it's much too late for them." said Mahdi.

"Ask him, if we can do anything for the village."

"He says for us to leave."

"Tell him, I'm sorry." I said.

We return to the equipment on the adjacent hillside. The workers begin the refueling process as we prepare to start anew. We'll not stop until we reach El Geneina, on the Chadian border.

"Where are the food shipments, Mr. Richard?" asked Mahdi.

"Honestly, I haven't a clue."

"Do you think, they have stopped sending it?"

"I'm not sure about anything at this point."

"Do you think it's necessary to continue to El Geneina?"

"Mahdi, my orders are to open a road to El Geneina. We'll not stop before then."

"Thanks, Mr. Richard, for not giving up."

"I want both dozers out in front today."

"O.K." said Mahdi.

"Let's move out."

A new year comes and goes, as we continue to press toward the village of Kebkabiya. For over 2 months we've seen no food shipments. We're surviving entirely off the land now. We have only mango and guava for food. We have emptied one of the large fuel tankers. We have only one left to continue the road building.

We arrive at the empty village of Kebkabiya, in February, it's people having fled to El Geneina, in search of food. We camp for the night and move out at daybreak. The crew desperately needing food and medical attention, refuse to stop.

Suddenly, a roar is coming from the skies. It's the sound of propellers, beating against the wind.

"What's that sound, Mr. Richard?"

"Helicopters." I answered.

Looking from the southeast, 3 large double propeller, Chinook helicopters flew directly overhead. Hanging beneath them were large cargo nets, filled with grain. A cheer goes up from the crew knowing food is arriving in El Geneina.

The giant red and white helicopters, have given us hope, that the relief operation continues. Those brief moments, as the helicopters flew overhead, added comfort to our miserable condition.

"Who's helicopters are those?" asked Mahdi.

"They're not Arkel-Talab." I answered.

"Maybe the American military?"

"No, those belong to a civilian company."

"How can you tell?" he asked.

"The American military doesn't ride around in red and white helicopters."

"The crew is very excited about seeing the food, as it passed over." he said.

"Tell the crew we should be arriving in El Geneina in a few days."

"I'll pass the word." said Mahdi.

Each morning, the bright helicopters fly overhead en-route to El Geneina. Their cargo nets stuffed to capacity with grain. I see and feel the excitement growing, as we draw closer to the town.

El Geneina, land with a sultan, sits along the border of Chad. This small town is harboring several hundred thousand refugees in search for food. It will be the final resting place for many, located 1,000 kilometers west of Khartoum. It lies on the very edge of the Sahara desert.

Members from 12 tribes inhabit this border town. The problem now is to provide food, clothing, and shelter in an effort to keep them alive.

Many refugees sleep on the ground, with little more than branches for shelter. Temperatures often drop to below 5 degrees centigrade at night.

Three helicopters are arriving with additional grain. They begin lowering their cargo nets in the center of an open area.

I began to wonder, what good is the road if the food is being flown into El Geneina. Maybe this was a wasted trip, after all. I've seen no ground shipments in several months. I had received orders to build a pioneer road from El Fasher to El Geneina. Within a couple of days, it will be completed. I have received no further orders, so I'll have no choice but return to Nyala.

We're several miles from town, and the hillsides and valleys are covered with thousands of temporary shelters. We pass tens of thousands of famine ravished people, lying about the area. The people are so abundant in number we have to turn the equipment around, and secure it several miles outside the town.

"Leave 2 people to watch the equipment. The others will go with us to obtain food."

We enter the city with two trucks, and find the food being distributed by the EEC. The police are using camel whips to keep the people in line. They issue the crew several sacks of grain. The crew returns to the equipment as Mahdi and I walk through the mass Exodus.

"How many people do you think are here?" asked Mahdi.

"Several hundred thousand at least." I answered.

"Do you think the helicopters can fly enough food to feed this many people?"

"No, it'll take several hundred tons to keep them alive."

"Do you believe they'll start sending convoys, now that we've finished the road?"

"If they don't use the road, thousands more will parish."

The flies are crawling on everything in sight. The poor people are lying on the ground for miles covered with flies.

The smell is unbearable as we make our way through the crowded streets.

"Look over here Mr. Richard." said Mahdi.

I walk over to see what he had found. It was a large stack of dead bodies, covered with flies. A group of people were digging a large hole nearby, to bury them.

"Will you take a picture of this so you'll remember this day?" he asked.

"Mahdi, I'll never forget this day. No, I won't take a picture, because I never want to see this again."

Only dried flesh, pressing against bone, could describe the horrific sight. Many of the dead, with eyes wide open, remind the living of their fate.

We make our way to a small tent with a sign reading, Doctors without Borders. Inside, I find several Europeans, fighting desperately to save the sick and dying. Though small in number, their courage is to be heralded. One of the doctors, watches as we enter, ran over and introduced himself.

"I'm Geoffrey, with the EEC." he said.

"I'm Field Supervisor with Arkel-Talab." I responded.

"You're the one everyone's looking for." he said.

"I don't follow you." I said.

"Arkel-Talab has been trying to locate you for several months. They didn't know if you were still alive?"

"If they wanted to know my whereabouts, they should have issued me a radio." I answered.

"They have been in radio contact with us for the past three months, asking if you've arrived."

"When you speak to them again, tell them we're awaiting new orders."

"I'll call them now." he said.

"Is the road open to El Geneina?" he asked.

"Yes, we pushed through today."

"We've got a large convoy ready to leave El Fasher. I'll radio them to head this way." he said.

He ran to the radio and began to speak to his men in El Fasher. Within minutes, he returned saying, "The convoy is en-route at this very moment."

Jubilation could be heard throughout the tent. Everyone was rejoicing that the main element of food was on the way. He returned to the radio and began to speak.

"Hello Nyala, Come in Arkel-Talab."

"Hello, this is Ronnie with Arkel-Talab in Nyala."

"Yes, This is Doctors Without Borders in El Geneina. We have your Field Supervisor with us. Do you wish to speak to him?"

"Yes, yes, put him on the radio." said Ronnie.

"Hello Ronnie, I'm waiting for further instructions."

"Your instructions are to return to Nyala, now!" he shouted.

"You sound like this is an emergency."

"Everyone thought you were dead. No one could find you."

"What about the equipment?"

"Send everything you've got to Nyala." he said.

"We'll leave today. It'll be several days before we arrive."

"Just one more thing. You better keep a low profile on the road. I'll explain that to you later." he said.

"O.K. El Geneina, out."

"Thanks for opening the road between us and El Fasher." the doctor said.

"You deserve the thanks, for what you're doing out here." I replied.

"Please be careful around the villagers. We're finding cholera, malaria, dysentery and a host of other diseases."

"We're staying beyond arms length at all times." I said.

"Please be careful on your return trip. We've heard refugees talking about bandits in the hill country."

"We've already had our share of bandits."

"Do you plan to stay here tonight?"

"No, we're leaving now. Thanks for everything."

We head directly to the equipment to begin the long trek home.

"Have the men saddle up."

"I'll have them ready as soon as we refuel." said Mahdi.

One last look at the thousands of refugees covering the hills and plains. It's mind boggling at how well the few EEC members maintain order. They deserve a 'well done' to their arduous task, under such extreme conditions.

"Mr. Richard, what did Ronnie mean, when he said to keep a low profile on the return trip?"

"I don't know, Mahdi."

"Maybe he thinks the villagers don't like the road coming so close to them?"

"Maybe."

"He sounded as if something big has happened."

"It took something huge to get their attention, for sure."

"What do you think will happen when we reach Nyala?" asked Mahdi.

"We'll just have to wait and see."

We're traveling at top speed on our newly completed road.

The tank carriers are an asset, as they carry the two large dozers. We travel as far as Kebkabyia, and camp for the night.

"Do you think they're angry at us for taking the dozers in Dei?" asked Mahdi.

"If they are, we'll tell the general. Don't sweat the small stuff, I'm prepared to take the blame."

"I want to be with you, when you arrive at the office."

"I wouldn't have it any other way."

"Mr. Richard, why did you come to Sudan? Was it because of the famine relief?"

"No, I'm going to be honest with you. I had no idea there was a famine in Sudan, until I talked to someone in the airport in Frankfurt, Germany."

"Then, why did you come to Sudan?"

"I came for adventure."

"Did you find it?"

"Yes, more than I bargained for."

"Do the people in America know what's going on in my country?"

"No, I'm afraid not."

"Why aren't they aware of our situation?"

"Because, they're to busy playing golf, and making money."

"You'll be going home now."

"Yes, I believe my time is at hand to depart."

"Will you ever return?"

"No, I'm afraid not."

"The crew says you're a good Quawagi. They like you very much."

"You tell the entire crew, it was an honor working with them."

"We will miss you for a long time."

"I'll never forget the people of Sudan and their terrible plight to survive."

"We shall always be grateful for your sacrifice."

"Mahdi, your people are the ones who've sacrificed."

"You gave more than we could ask."

"I wish I could have done more."

"We could not take more from you."

"Thanks for everything, Mahdi."

The morning brings the sound of engines as we prepare to leave. We take the lead, as the giant tank carriers follow close behind. We travel several hours, without meeting the convoy. We arrive at Omri, at mid-afternoon before seeing dust rising in the distance.

"Stop. We'll wait on them here." I said.

Within minutes a large convoy of 20 souk trucks arrive. A man emerges from the lead vehicle, and begins waving for us to join him. He's British, male, in his mid-thirties from the EEC.

"Have you heard the news, mate?" he asked.

"What news?" I asked.

"The United States attacked Libya, and they're at war." he said.

"When did this happen?" I asked.

"Yesterday. All relief workers have been ordered out of this area." he said.

"Do you mind if we look at your cargo?" I asked.

"No, go right ahead."

"Let's have one last look, Mahdi." I said.

"What are you guys looking for, anyway?" he asked.

"Nuclear waste." I answered.

"Nuclear waste! Are you crazy?" he shouted.

"Yes, crazy like a fox." I said.

"Look, fellows, we've got to unload in El Geneina tonight. We've got to go." he said.

"Have a safe trip, sir." I replied.

"Thank you." he said.

We watch the long convoy proceed toward El Geneina. It will not feed the multitude we had witnessed for more than a week. The war in neighboring Libya spelled disaster for the relief effort.

Mahdi, tell the soldiers to proceed to Nyala, with the equipment, and we'll meet them there."

"They said, they'll be there in a couple of days."

"We'll bypass El Fasher, just in case there's Libyan sympathizers in the area." I said.

"I agree. We'll cut through the hills, and avoid everyone." said Mahdi.

We watch the equipment as it disappears in the distance. We turn south, heading into the barren wilderness once again. We travel several hours without encountering anyone. We stop at a small wadi, searching for water. Within a half hour we're traveling once again, through rugged terrain. Several hours have passed, as darkness falls once again in western Darfur. We camp along a hillside, several miles from the nearest village.

"Mr. Richard, why is America attacking Libya?"

"Because they have hijacked a number of our airplanes, killing several innocent civilians."

"Why are they doing that?"

"Politics, religion, and a host of other differences which we don't even understand."

"Do you think they'll try and hijack your plane going home?"

"No, I don't think they'll be hijacking any more planes, for a while."

"Do you think the relief operation in Darfur was a cover-up for something larger?" asked Mahdi.

"Yes. The reporter went through a lot of trouble trying to contact us. He said his information came through channels in Washington, about the nuclear waste. I've been given the runaround since day one.

The company consistently refuses us access to a radio. Then the request by a high level official, to split the crew at Zalingei. Then came the order, to leave the dozers in remote Dei, to men who called themselves doctors. If this were a legitimate operation there would have been at least a dozen road crews in this area. There was no need in waiting until thousands had died to begin the relief effort, especially during the rainy season." I answered.

"Will we ever know?" asked Mahdi.

"Your future generations will know for sure."

"What do you want to do?"

"Tomorrow morning , we'll detour through the village of Dei, for one final look."

"O.K. Mr. Richard, it'll be good for both of us."

At daylight we head south across no mans land. The carcasses of many animals litter the hillsides, as we make our way toward the village. We stop at a dry creek bed in search of water, finding none. We continue south, hoping to arrive at the village by noon.

"Over that ridge Mahdi."

"O.K." he said.

"Stop! That's the exact spot the 2 men wanted the dozers left."

"It looks so different Mr. Richard."

"Yes, The entire area has been leveled and reconstructed."

"They have moved tons of dirt, in order to cover this area." said Mahdi.

"Apparently, they found their own dozers."

An area the size of a football field had been elevated, and covered several feet deep with laterite. The flat area we had left earlier, now resembled an American Indian mound. We walk over the entire structure, built since we had left, months before. The project must have taken several weeks to complete. Whoever built this pyramid style structure, had picked the most remote place on earth, in which to carry out their operation. I only wished I had stayed around to watch the show.

"What do you think, Mr. Richard?" asked Mahdi.

"If this is a graveyard, it's the largest one in Sudan?"

"It's not a graveyard, is it, Mr. Richard?"

"No, it's not."

"What do you want to do?"

"We're not going to dig inside to find out, like the reporters." I answered.

"I think you're right about the cover up, Mr. Richard."

"There's nothing we can do now. Let's go home Mahdi."

We pass through the village of Dei, and the people wave as we continue south. We cross the Gabian bridge for the last time at Zalingei. We'll be in Nyala in a few hours. We stop only once for water, so we can arrive before dark. The sun begins hiding behind the hills, as we enter Nyala, for the first time in many months. We weave through the crowed streets as we near the office of Arkel-Talab. We pull inside the walled complex, and exit the vehicle.

"Watch out Mahdi, there's a baboon around here somewhere."

"What's the reason for the baboon?"

"He's Ronnie's yard dog!"

Suddenly, the door opens and a voice calls from inside, "Richard, welcome home!" shouted Ronnie.

"I wasn't ready to come home. What's going on Ronnie?"

"The U.S. bombed Libya several days ago, and everyone has been ordered out of Sudan."

"What about the relief operation?"

"It's over."

"What about the equipment?"

"When it arrives you'll begin demobilization. Everything must be returned to Kosti."

"The equipment will arrive tomorrow morning."

"You'll have to make a report for everything that's happened out there."

"What kind of report?"

"You'll tell every single thing you've encountered, in the bush. Include the amount of miles covered, basically, everything you know."

"Who gets the final report?"

"It'll go to the U.S. Congress for evaluation. Their paying for the entire operation."

"I would like to take the map I borrowed, back to the EEC."

"It's to late, they've already evacuated the city."

"Why the rush to leave?"

"Several missionaries have been murdered in the last 2 months. There's plenty of anti-American sentiment in the area."

"Yes, I can see why."

The following morning the equipment is demobilized, and sent toward Kosti. I make out the final report explaining the 700 kilometers[420-miles] of road built during the relief operation.

"An American C-130 aircraft is en-route to pick you up, and return you to Khartoum." said Ronnie.

"Will you be going with me?"

"No, it'll take a couple more days to close this office."

"Ronnie, a C-130 aircraft is kind of expensive to be picking up one passenger."

"Yes, there'll be someone on board to debrief you."

"Why do I need to be debriefed?"

"It's happening to all of us."

"Who are these guys doing the debriefing?"

"Look, I just work here. I don't know anything more than that."

"Look Ronnie, I'd like some real answers before I leave."

"What would you like to know?"

"I'd like to know what the newspaper reporter was looking for?"

"I have no idea."

"I'd also like to know what those 2 guys, posing as doctors were doing in Dei?"

"I have more questions than answers. You'll have to ask someone else."

"I have to give you guys credit for keeping me in the dark."

"Look Richard, just go home and forget about this place."

"No, I won't forget."

I turn to Mahdi, who had been my interpreter, and faithful friend. I notice the sadness in his face, as he tries to speak. It would have been a real nightmare without his assistance.

"It's time to say goodbye, Mr. Richard."

"I'm afraid so, my friend. I appreciate all you've done for me. May we always be friends."

"You'll always be my friend, Mr. Richard."

"Thank you Jesus!" I said.

"Thank you Jesus." he replied.

"Take care my friend."

"Goodbye, Mr. Richard."

The aircraft circled the office as it made it's approach into Nyala. I load my bag into the land rover for the last ride through the town. We arrive within 10 minutes as the giant plane circles the sandy runway. The engines never shut down as a man waves for me to come aboard.

"Thanks for everything, Ronnie."

"Anytime, Richard."

As I walk toward the aircraft, I notice it has no markings on the exterior. Nothing to distinguish what nation it belongs to. Safely inside, I'm escorted to the cockpit. I'm strapped into a bench seat behind the pilot. A man straps himself next to me, as the plane begins taking off.

Within a few seconds we're airborne. The crew in the cockpit refuse to look at me, or acknowledge my presence. I notice they never once make eye contact. Another man enters the cockpit and straps himself in, on my right side.

"Are you guys with Air America?" I asked.

"I'm a Frenchmen." he replied.

"The guys in the cockpit look American."

"Yes, the pilot, co-pilot and flight engineer are all American."

"What are you guy's doing out here?" I asked.

"We're trying to evacuate all Americans from the country."

"The pilots aren't in uniform." I said.

"These guys have over a 100 years of total flying time. You're in good hands."

After a few moments of silence, he began to question me in length about the operation.

"Who are you?"

"I'm an American citizen."

"Who are you working for?"

"Arkel-Talab."

"How did you find out about Arkel-Talab?"

"They found me."

"What were you doing out here?" he asked.

"Building roads." I answered.

"What was the purpose of the roads?"

"Grain shipments." I answered.

"How long have you been here?"

"Several months."

"Did any of the villagers seem hostile?"

"No."

"Where you ever threatened?"

"No."

"Did you notice anything subversive?"

"No."

The debriefing lasted for most of the 3 hour flight. We circle the airport in Khartoum, twice before landing. I grab my bag and exit the aircraft not knowing what to expect. A Sudanese man waves for me to join him.

"Mr. Richard, I'll take you to the office."

"Thank you."

Within 30 minutes, I walk into the Khartoum office. A secretary hands over my passport and instructions on receiving my pay.

"Your pay is located in the Lloyds Bank in London. Upon arrival in the United States, your bank must submit this information, requesting a bank draft for your pay. Please sign this sheet of paper." she said.

"When is my flight scheduled to leave?"

"Tonight, at 10 P.M."

"Will someone be available to carry me to the airport?"

"Yes, be prepared to leave at 8P.M."

"I'll be ready."

I dig into the bottom of my bag and locate the clothes needed for the return trip home. I take up several belt holes to adjust for the 70 lbs. I'd lost in the desert. The trip proved to be an excellent weight loss program. I only wish I could have lost the weight under different circumstances.

The driver unloads my bag at the airport, and carries it inside. He places it at the ticket counter and wishes me a safe trip.

The military personnel began a final search of my bag. They took the bible out first, as they commence digging into every corner of the large suitcase. They return the bible, and stack the bag along side the loading ramp.

The two hour wait passed very quickly as the giant 747 landed on the tarmac. Only a handful of people exit the plane, and a small number climbed aboard. Within minutes, we're airborne and en-route to Cairo, Frankfurt, and the United States.

I watch the lights of Khartoum fade in the distance as I began gathering my thoughts. It'll be many years before I forget about the horrific ordeal, I had witnessed in Western Darfur.

I'll never forget the many faces of pain and suffering. The cries of innocent people, that go unheeded. The carcasses of people, strewn about, unknown to the world.

Only time will tell if they're threatened in a more subversive way.

THE END

About the Author

Dr. Richard C. Fennell
Doctor of Divinity
Doctor of Theology
Sgt. U.S. Marine Corps - Vietnam
U.S. Merchant Marine Licensed Engineer
National Association of Investigative Specialists